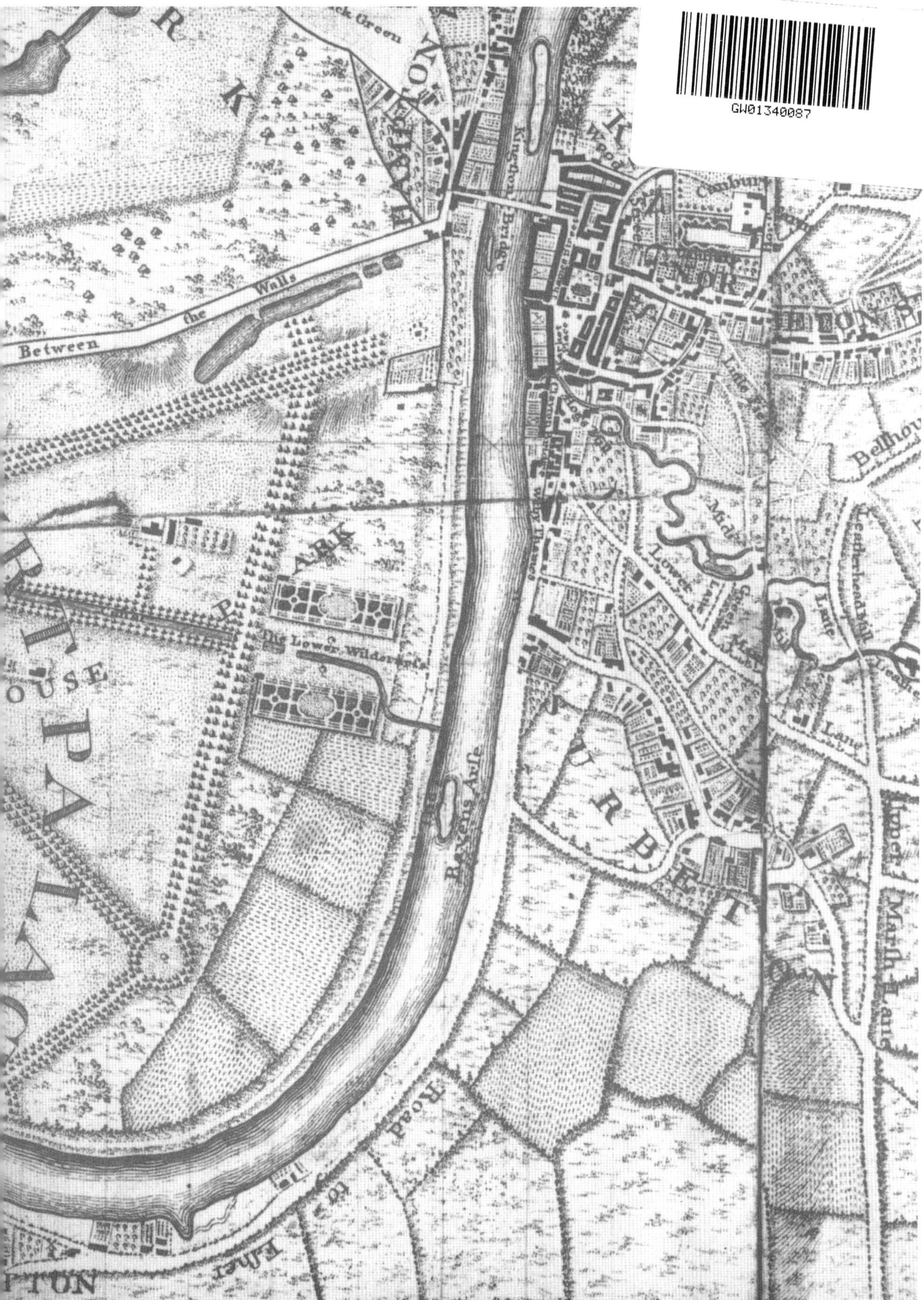
Between the Walls
Kingston Bridge
PARK
The Lower Wilderness
HOUSE
PALACE
Esher Road
Lower
Lane
Marsh Lane
Bellhou

THE BOOK OF MOLESEY

FRONT COVER: Hampton Court bridge in 1753. The Castle Hotel on the left hand side has a sign which proves that it was then called The Prince of Wales.

George Alderton (Capt) and members of East Molesey Fire Brigade, 1897.

THE BOOK OF MOLESEY

BY

ROWLAND G. M. BAKER

BARON
Buckingham
MMVI

Originally published in 1986
Second impression 1987
Third impression 2006
Fourth impression 2006

PUBLISHED BY BARON BOOKS OF BUCKINGHAM
IN THIS FOURTH IMPRESSION
PRODUCED BY THE BATH PRESS AND
ACADEMIC + TECHNICAL TYPESETTING

© Rowland G. M. Baker

All rights reserved. No part of this publication may be reproduced, stored in a retrieval system, or transmitted, in any form or by any means, electronic, mechanical, photocopying, recording or otherwise, without the prior permission of Baron Books.

Any copy of this book issued by the Publisher as clothbound or as a paperback is sold subject to the condition that it shall not by way of trade or otherwise, be lent, re-sold, hired out or otherwise circulated without the Publisher'r prior consent, in any form of binding or condition including this condition being imposed on a subsequent purchaser.

ISBN 0 86023 251 4

Contents

ACKNOWLEDGEMENTS	8
FOREWORD BY T. E. C. WALKER FSA	8
INTRODUCTION	9
ON SIMPLICITY BY JOSEPH BUDWORTH	10
FROM SMALL BEGINNINGS	12
MANORIAL MOLESEY	17
TUDOR TIMES	23
INTO SUBURBIA	26
HERE IS THE CHURCH	49
FOLK MOOT TO BOROUGH	59
FOR THE PEOPLE	66
HONEST TOIL	79
MANY MANSIONS	88
THERE IS A TAVERN	108
BIBLIOGRAPHY	122
INDEX	124

Acknowledgements

Anybody who ventures into the realm of local history must inevitably be beholden for the assistance provided by our public libraries and record offices. From famous national collections down to little local branches, librarians and archivists seem always helpful, always willing, always courteous. The author would like particularly to mention the following institutions: Molesey Library, Kingston Heritage Centre, Surrey Record Office, Surrey Local Studies Library, Guildhall Library, Minet Library, Greater London Record Office, Public Record Office, British Library, and Colindale Newspaper Library. Will the staff of each and all of them, and of many others whose aid I have solicited over the years, please accept my sincere thanks for their assistance and encouragement?

I would also express my obligation to our local ministers, Rev W. A. J. Yeend of West Molesey, and Rev E. C. Allen of East Molesey, and to the Clerk of the old Esher UDC, for allowing me access to the books and papers within their care.

Most of all, however, must I express my indebtedness to the various people of Molesey, who in the fifty or so years during which I have delved into the history of the two villages, have told me of their lives in the past, have shown me their cherished possessions, allowed me into and to photograph their homes, let me see their deeds, and to copy their old pictures. They are far too numerous for me to mention individually by name. Sadly, many are no longer with us. The rest will probably recognise themselves and their contributions to this work. I hope they will take this as my unfeigned gratitude for all their kind help and support.

Finally I would acknowledge my thanks to Mr Conway Walker (who was recently described as the doyen of local history) for writing the foreword to this book; and to Mr Clive Birch of Barracuda Books, who first suggested its production.

NOTE TO FOURTH IMPRESSION
This impression has been published by kind permission of the author's widow, Mrs Gwen Baker, and with the assistance of her son, Steve Baker, and made possible by the Molesey Residents Association and its members.

Foreword

by T. E. C. Walker FSA

Every town and village should have its local history worthily recorded, by a qualified writer. Rowland Baker has now done this for Molesey. No single volume can thoroughly cover all aspects of the subject, and we look forward to another book from Mr Baker at some future time. The author has my congratulations for the work he has already done.

Dedication

For Gwendoline Freda

Introduction

'No retrospect will take us to the true beginning;
and whether our prologue be in heaven or on earth,
it is but a fraction of that all-presupposing fact
with which our story sets out'.
George Eliot, *Daniel Deronda* (1876)

Why is this work entitled *The Book of Molesey* when, as some people will be quick to point out, there are two Moleseys — East and West? Originally there was only one settlement, *Molesey*, for, as Professor Maitland has stated 'Men did not make two contiguous villages and call them both by the same name. Names are given to places in order that they may be distinguished from neighbouring places. So when we see two different villages both called X lying next to each other, we may be fairly certain that they are not of equal antiquity, and it is not unlikely that the one is the offshoot and daughter of the other'. In Molesey the prefixes East and West did not appear until about the year 1200, before when there was only one parish, and we can be fairly certain that that was centred around what we now call East Molesey, and that West Molesey was its daughter.

After the creation of West Molesey, the two places continued their separate identities, administratively until 1895, when they were united under one local council, and visually till the years between the wars, when residential development marched steadily across the map until the two villages coalesced. So that nowadays, in looking at the streets and houses, nothing is left to betray where one parish ends and the other begins. Still more confusing is the fact that the one thing which used to demonstrate the border — the boundary stone set up in 1866 — was re-erected some time ago in the wrong position. With continual reorganisation and amalgamation of local government units there remains no administrative function dependent upon the time-honoured parochial bounds; even the wards into which the present Borough is split are fashioned for convenience of voting rather than on anything historical.

Furthermore, the story of the places is so intermingled that one could not possibly tell one without continual reference to the other. For the benefit of this work, therefore, the two are recorded together, and *Molesey* is used throughout instead of the more cumbersome *East* and *West Molesey*, whenever reference to the whole district is intended.

The perspective as it is viewed today is the outcome of the collective contributions of many, many generations of human occupation. Each generation amended the fabric according to its needs, ability, and accumulated experience, adding, as it were, a touch of its own identity to the final tableau. It is the intention of the author, therefore, primarily to try and identify some of the historical factors which have produced this kaleidoscope we now call Molesey.

The two villages lie side by side along the banks of one of the most pleasant stretches of the river Thames, on the northern boundary of the county of Surrey, twelve miles from the centre of London, and within the Borough of Elmbridge.

The area of East Molesey consists of 781 acres of land and 38 of water; West Molesey of 658 acres of land and 81 of water; a grand total of 1,558 acres. This makes them, for reasons which will be considered later, two of the smallest parishes in the whole of Surrey.

There are no striking geographical features, with little or no ground rising above thirty or so feet. Nevertheless, the views 'along the shore of silver streaming Thames', towards the gables of Hampton and the mighty pile of Hampton Court, are not indeed unpleasing; neither are the walks along the banks of the river Mole, to 'Claremont's terraced height and Esher's groves'. Further to the south may be traced the blue outline of the Surrey Hills. The parishes of Thames Ditton, Esher, and Walton-on-Thames lie respectively to the east, south, and west.

On Simplicity

Written on the banks of the river Mole on 15 January 1800, by Joseph Budworth, afterwards Joseph Palmer (1765-1815).

Dear Peaceful Molesey, ever in my mind
Thou shalt a niche of recollection find;
Her showy meadows and elastic air,
Which Thames they loved borders share,
Her fields luxuriant in autumnal grain,
Bending beneath the plenty they contain;
Her stacks of riches, an the numerous sheep,
Which to the wether-bell due orders keep,
While the old shepherd toddles to his tree,
Attended by his cluster'd family;
Then underneath its foliage recline,
Pull out his scrip, and with contentment dine.
Her wealthy yeomen, an industrious race!
For centuries past the heirlooms of the place:
And husbandmen so wedded to their soil,
Who ne'er have changed their village, or their toil;
Rough children on their humble hearths abound,
And ripe old age with healthful wrinkles crown'd.
The Thames, majestic! flowing by her side,
Where num'rous swans in stately freedom glide:
The willow'd Aytes their annual nests contain,
Where undisturbed the mother birds remain.
The little Mole, which lingers through her fields,
To many mills proverbial plenty yields;
So grieves to leave·them, she forsakes her bed,
And in the monarch's bosom hides her head.
Say, why should we our little Mole prefer?
It is the unfetter'd quiet reigning there.
Oh sweet simplicity! thou gen'rous maid!
That decks with matchless charms the rural shade.
Thine is the gift to live and laugh with ease,
And, like thy parent Nature, ever please.

ABOVE: The old rustic bridge — Tanners Bridge, before river widening. BELOW: River Bank on a busy Edwardian summer Sunday.

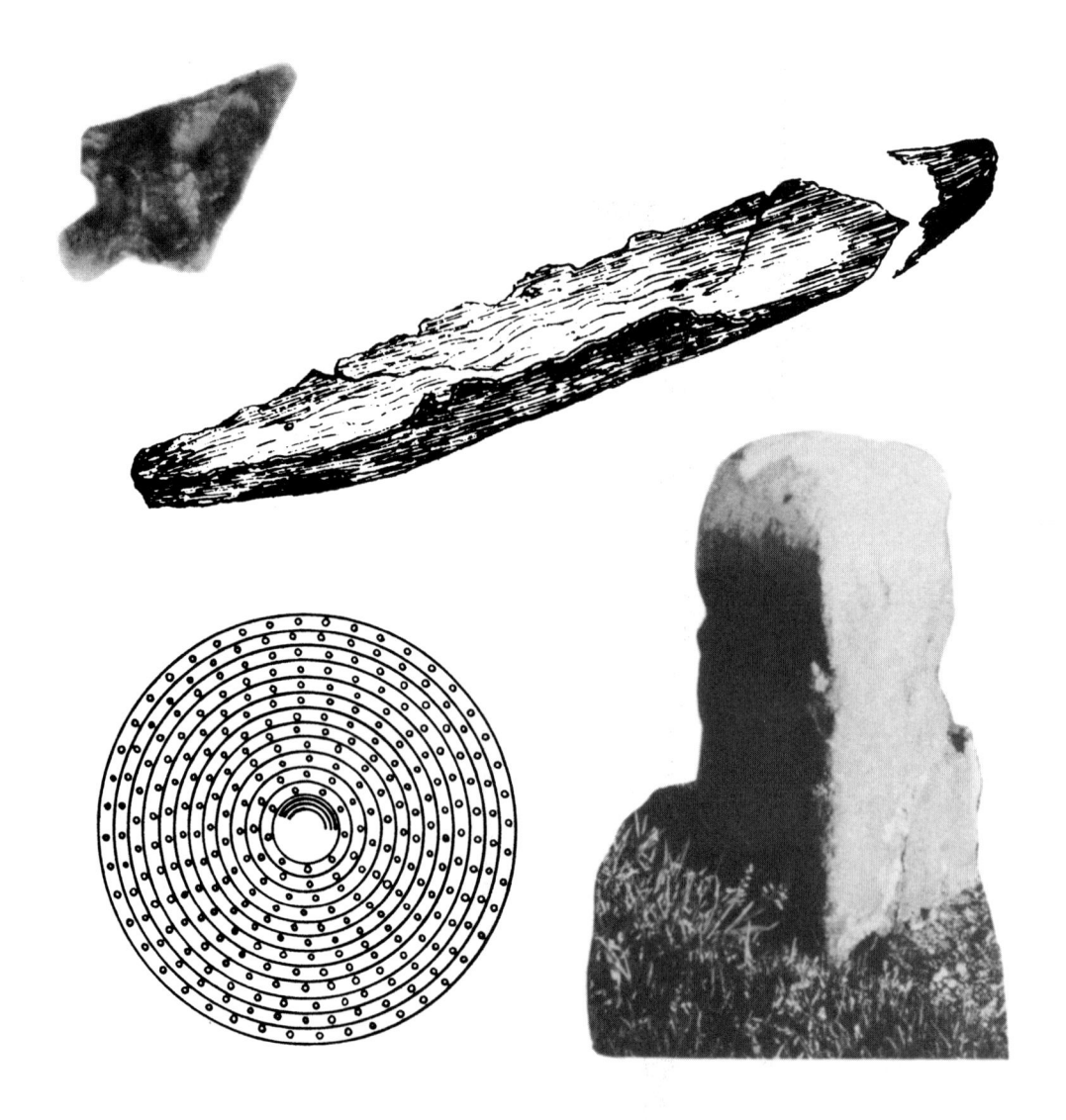

ABOVE LEFT: Flint arrowhead, found in the gravel in East Molesey. RIGHT: Dug-out log canoe, probably from the Iron Age, recovered from the river bed at West Molesey. Originally about 15 feet long and two feet eight inches wide, by the time of its discovery much had eroded away. BELOW LEFT: Well-ornamented circular bronze shield from the Bronze Age, excavated from the river bed at West Molesey. RIGHT: Boundary stone, erected in 1865, between the parishes of East and West Molesey.

From Small Beginnings

'Mighty things from small beginnings grow'
John Dryden, *Annus Mirabilis* (1666/7)

The primary constituent which moulds an individual locality is undoubtedly its relationship to the natural physical domain on which it stands; the fundamental geography which shaped Molesey's destiny and enduring character — and to which we shall return time and time again throughout this narrative — is the water which surrounds it, and from which it is impossible to escape.

It was a sub-tropical sea, perhaps some fifty million years ago, which deposited the underlying foundation of thick tenacious clay, the basis of our sub-soil. It was the swirling waters of a mighty river, probably a melting glacier, the last remnants of the time when Britain was shrouded in the frigidity of an ice-age, which precipitated the broad stratum of gravel which overlies the clay, and which, as sand and ballast, is extracted as builder's material today. After the last glacial period, when the retreating ice finally departed this country, the rushing current gradually subsided, leaving the gentler flowing Thames slowly to cut its tortuous course to the sea.

It was the Thames and its tributaries, not only the Mole and the Ember, but at one time also innumerable brooks and rivulets that fed into them, which laid down their sediment to form the alluvial, rich and fertile soils, that spread themselves atop the surface of the area.

In the gravel and soft soil of the river alluvium are sometimes found the fossilised remains of the creatures which lived here millions of years ago. For instance, when the foundations for the hotel on Tagg's Island were excavated about 1857, some seventeen feet below the surface several specimens were found, including the skull of a long since extinct species of goat, and the jaw bone of a large boar's head.

The natural virgin landscape that arose upon this indigenous low-lying structure, devoid of Man's influencing hand, would have been a covering of heavy forest trees, thick alderwood, willow, and the like, interspersed with an entanglement of dense reedy undergrowth, liable at all times to frequent and persistent disgorges of floodwater.

Such land formed a redoubtable obstacle to the earliest of our ancestors, much too inhospitable and uninviting for their settlement. The simple folk of primeval times sought instead an open upland terrain where they could scratch away with their primitive wooden implements at the light easily workable soils: a vantage point, readily defensible, with elevated views over the countryside, whereon they might not suddenly be surprised either by intruding enemies or marauding animals, and free from the scourge of disease which could attack either themselves or their flocks in the dank nether region below.

Nevertheless, conditions suitable for their choice were to be found not far away on the ridge of sand hills to the south of Molesey, and a string of prehistoric settlements certainly existed upon these hills, on the Warren at Esher, on St George's Hill at Walton, on St Anne's Hill at Chertsey, and on Wimbledon Common. Further to the south of this line of hill forts, and forming a formidable barrier to other settlements, was a broad area of thick clay, marshy and impenetrably wooded. Access to and from these communities, therefore, was virtually only possible on and along the rivers which early man used as his main means of travel. The Thames and the Mole soon emerged as most important factors in communication. In consequence, it is not surprising that all the relics which pre-Iron Age Man left in our area have been dredged from the beds of rivers. The character of these finds, notably not less than three log canoes, hacked out of solid tree trunks, which were sunk in the river bed to be preserved in the mud and brought out for our inspection some two or three thousand years later, is a significant reminder that our earliest visitors were merely travellers along these watery highways, and not permanently settled inhabitants. Other artefacts which have been excavated from the rivers include an axe from the Stone Age and a flint dagger, a spearhead, a looped palstave, and a magnificently embossed shield, from the Bronze Age.

The drift away from the old hill forts into the river valleys, which is sometimes referred to as the valleyward movement, started in the late Iron Age, say in the 1st century BC. Probably under the influence of immigrant Belgic tribes, it continued during Roman and Anglo-Saxon times. Its causes were due, first to a much greater sense of security and political stability, and secondly, and more particularly, to higher technical skills, especially the improved iron industry, producing stronger iron axes for the formidable task of clearing the dense woodland, and allowing the development of the heavy wheeled plough with iron share and coulter, enabling the tougher, more fertile, soils of the river valleys thus cleared to be exploited.

It is not certain exactly when the area now forming Mosesey first became permanently inhabited. Probably, at first land communication in the valleys strayed not too far from the river banks. In the Lower Mole Valley it seems almost certain that a trackway ran close to the river, at least from Cobham to the Thames. Recent excavations adjacent to the Mole, at Southwood Manor Farm at Hersham, prove that a settlement existed there which was occupied during the Iron Age and up to Roman times, and a road broadly following the banks of the river was in use between Hersham and Cobham, until the beginning of the nineteenth century. It was abandoned when new roads were laid out when the commons were enclosed.

The earliest occupants of Molesey, therefore, probably established themselves alongside this road, on the slightly rising ground in the wide sweep of the river Mole on which St Mary's Church now stands. (Remember that, even during the disastrous inundation of 1968, St Mary's stood on an island of dry land, environed all round by a sea of flood water). From here they gradually spread out into the surrounding country.

There remains no archaeological or historical evidence to prove the rate at which colonisation of the area took place, either during the Iron Age or in the subsequent Roman occupation, or to show continuity with the flourishing community which undoubtedly existed here in Saxon times. The Saxon invaders, as Sir Cyril Fox describes, 'preferred the deep meadow to the hill-pasture; and were probably the first people in Britain to bring order into the marshy alder-choked alluvium of our lowland valley floors' — an apt description of Molesey at that time. This period, then, marked a great step forward, from a people subject entirely to the physical environment in which they dwelt, to one which could at least in some way control its own progress and destiny.

The area under occupation soon increased but, because of the ever-encompassing rivers, which were hemmed in by other and more ancient communities, the settlement was not encircled, as most villages are, by waste lands, and once cultivation reached these boundaries, no further expansion was possible. Thus the Moleseys remain to this day as two of the smallest parishes in the whole of Surrey.

The earliest documentary evidence relating to this settlement in Molesey stems from the mid-seventh century. At that time the land of Surrey stood amid powerful and contending neighbours, buffeted in turn by one and the other, each grappling for supremacy. Around the year AD 660 it came under the jurisdiction of Wulfhere, son of Penda the great king of Mercia, who installed a vassal ruler, one Frithwald, the only recorded sub-king of Surrey. Wulfhere was the first Mercian monarch to be baptised, and became an ardent protagonist of Christianity. Under his influence, the new religion was implanted in the territory, and the saintly Erkenwald, later to become Bishop of London, was installed as his missionary.

About the year 666, 'through love of heavenly glory', Erkenwald founded a monastery for Benedictine monks on a piece of sparsely inhabited land near the Thames at Chertsey, and dedicated it to St Peter. Shortly afterwards, Frithwald endowed it with a grant of much land in north-west Surrey, including *Mulesei*, with all the 'Fields, Woods, Meadows, Feeding, Rivers, and all other things rightly belonging thereto'. The rents from these lands were to be utilised in the construction and maintenance of the conventual buildings and for the sustenance of the monks. This grant was confirmed in a charter on which Frithwald 'on account of my ignorance of letters' expressed the sign of the holy cross. Chertsey Abbey's lordship over Molesey was thus secured, and by several subsequent ratifications was guaranteed for the next three hundred years and more. From these and later bequests, Chertsey grew to be one of the richest and most powerful abbeys in the whole of southern England.

Thereafter, little is heard of the Abbey or its Molesey possessions, until the second half of the ninth century. Then the peace of the countryside was rudely shattered by incursions of ravaging Vikings. In search of plunder they sailed their longships right up the Thames, past London, and on to Chertsey, where they pillaged the monastery of its treasures, set it alight, slaughtered the abbot and ninety of the brethren, and laid the country all around, undoubtedly including the land of Molesey, to waste.

Following this devastation and the loss of its productive estates, the monastery suffered a severe setback, and it was not until some fifty years had passed that, in the year 933, King Athelstan refounded the Abbey in a charter issued from the 'royal town called in English Kingston', which confirmed all the old possessions, including the lands at *Muleseige*, to the 'venerable community of Chertsey as have been constituted and confirmed to that honourable priory by our predecessors from ancient times'.

In the ensuing years, a general laxity overtook the Church, and Chertsey, like many other abbeys, was taken over by ordinary priests, who were not bound by rigorous monastic vows. The fabric was allowed to fall into disrepair, and King Edwy diverted at least some of the Abbey's property at Molesey to the Monastery of St Swithin at Winchester. In 964, Edwy's half brother Edgar, who had succeeded him, and was a young monarch passionately attached to the Christian church, was induced by his bishops to expel the priests and replace them with monks, over whom he appointed an abbot to maintain observance of strict monastic rule and discipline.

King Edgar also restored to the 'Full and quiet possession of the Abbey' all the land which they had previously owned, including 'twenty mansas in Muleseye which Edwy had unjustly diverted'.

However, some time during the following century, and at least by the reign of King Edward the Confessor (1042-1066), Molesey had been divided between four thanes, named respectively Aulric, Toco, Tovi, and Ullward; no records survive to explain why, when, and by whom, the land was taken away from Chertsey Abbey and conferred upon others.

PARISH OF
EAST MOLESEY,
SURREY,
14th AUGUST, 1858.

Pursuant to the subjoined requisition, and for the purposes therein mentioned, the Parishioners are hereby required to meet at the Bell Inn, East Molesey, on the 23rd day of September next, *at 7 p.m.*

J. BEBB, *Churchwarden.*

TO THE CHURCHWARDENS OF THE PARISH OF EAST MOULSEY, IN THE COUNTY OF SURREY.

You are hereby requested to summon a Vestry Meeting for the purpose of considering whether or not it will be advisable for the parish of East Moulsey and the district of Kent Town, both in the County of Surrey, to unite in erecting and maintaining a joint School for the Children of the Poor of East Moulsey aforesaid, and of the said district, and of determining what course to adopt in reference thereto.

Dated this thirty-first day of July, 1858.

Geo. Royer,	John Cann,	Thos. Edmonds,
Thos. Wills,	George Harrow,	James Heather,
B. W. Mullins,	Robert Hastings,	Thomas Smith,
E. Hopwood,	Jesse Wheatley,	W. B. Roberts,
J. Hoare,	Henry Weston,	G. E. Wood,
William Cozens,	George Betty,	J. Lane,
William Haynes	Henry Alderton,	Charles Davis.

Handbill, dated 1858, showing the indiscriminate use of the spellings
Molesey and *Moulsey* on the same document.

The earliest extant document on which the name of Molesey is recorded was in the charter endowing Chertsey Abbey, wherein it is spelled *Mulesei*, which etymologists suggest is derived from the personal name *Mul*, compounded with the Old English *ey*, meaning an island or river meadow — thus Mul's Island. Who, then, was this man Mul who is so remembered? There was a prince, brother of Cadwalla, King of Wessex, with this name, but there seems to be no evidence to connect him with this area and it is unlikely to have been him. The name was pronounced 'mule' and, like that hybrid animal, denoted the offspring of mixed parentage, probably of a Saxon father and a Celtic mother, and was fairly common. Probably the eponymous Mul will never be known.

In Domesday Book, the name was Normanised to Molesham. Mediaeval spellings are usually variations of the original Mulesey, or of Molesey, until about Tudor times, when Moulsey appears. This latter was much used by Victorians, together with the older Molesey, and sometimes both spellings appear in the same document. Gradually Molesey got the upper hand, and was finally adopted by the Post Office as the official spelling.

Manorial Molesey

'To whom the Lord of the Manor aforesaid by his
Steward Granted Seisin thereof By the Rod To Have
and to Hold to Him and his Heirs at the Will of
the Lord according to the Custom of the Manor'
   Molesey Matham manor court roll, 24 July 1771

After the Conqueror's decisive victory at Hastings, he marched his elated followers towards London but, not wishing to risk a frontal attack on a capital which proved less than submissive, settled instead on a broad outflanking manoeuvre, pushing his warriors on through Surrey, Hampshire, and Berkshire, cruelly harrying the countryside as they went. Molesey lay right in the path of this relentless host and, like the rest, was laid waste, its fields left destitute, its Saxon owners dispossessed. Indeed, when the time came for the spoils to be doled out to new Norman proprietors, as a reward for their conquering assistance, the value of the property was nearly halved.

Molesey was now bestowed upon two knights, Richard Fitzgilbert and Odard Balastarius, in return for certain specified military service for the King. Fitzgilbert, sometimes known as Richard de Tonbridge or Richard de Clare, was a kinsman of the Conqueror himself, and one of his closest companions, a powerful baron, who became chief justice of England, and was awarded many estates throughout the Kingdom. He was the founder of a family which in time embraced the Earldoms of Clare, Hertford, Pembroke, and Gloucester. It must be said, however, that Richard never occupied his manor of Molesey himself; in fact, it is doubtful that he ever set foot in it — he just owned it and let it out to lesser knights, from whom he exacted service in return.

Odard Balastarius was the officer in charge of the ballista, a large engine of war somewhat like a massive catapult, for hurling missiles on the ranks of the enemy. He is, therefore, sometimes referred to as the Engineer or the Crossbowman.

The Domesday Survey of 1086 lists the number of Saxon peasants who toiled on the land in Molesey as 23 *villeins*, men who tilled their own soil but were not free to go as they pleased and who were forced to work on the fields of the manorial lord for a certain number of days each year; 8 *bordars* and 9 *cottars*, who possessed no land except that immediately around their cottages and were even more rigidly tied to the manor, and 8 *serfs*, slaves who held no land at all, had no rights, and were the absolute property of the lord of the manor: a total of 48 men and, with women and children, the priest, the steward and other officials, yielding a community of, say 200 souls.

The descendants of Odard Balastarius held the manor for many years by the service of providing a crossbowman for the King's army for forty days a year, at their own cost, and thereafter at the King's cost. The name Simon Arbelastarius appears on a local document dated 1167, and W. Arbalastarius on another in 1206. Around this time, however, the family seem to have dropped the surname and adopted a territorial designation. For, in 1215 we find the manor held by Sampson de Molesey, later by his son and grandson, eventually devolving on his great-granddaughter, Isabella de Molesey, who married the owner of a small estate called Matham at Sawbridgeworth in Hertfordshire. Her husband, John de Matham, succeeded in her right, since when this manor has always been referred to as the manor of Molesey Matham.

After passing through several generations, the property was divided in 1455 among three daughters. Parts were subsequently re-united, but it settled down into two distinct and separate manors, which were known respectively as the manor of *Molesey Matham or East Molesey* and the manor of *Molesey Matham or West Molesey*; neither of these were co-extensive with the parishes of East Molesey or West Molesey, and both contained lands in adjacent parishes.

During the reign of Henry VIII both these manors, like all the surrounding ones, were acquired by the Crown to form a vast forest or hunting chase and, when no longer required for this purpose, were leased to various tenants, mostly courtiers or servants of the Royal court who desired an estate in the vicinity of Hampton Court.

In 1632, after some years of being let out in this fashion on short leases, the freehold of the East Molesey manor was sold by Charles I (ever in need of ready cash) to Ralph Freeman, a rich London merchant, who re-sold it for a profit in the following year to Sir John Lytcott, a gentleman of the privy chamber. Sir John is buried in St Mary's Church, where his monument, together with several to members of the Clarke family who followed him, may still be seen.

At the end of the 18th century, Joseph Clarke, the then lord of the manor, who was apparently somewhat of a rake and man-about-town and frittered away the fortune his forbears worked so hard to acquire, first mortgaged the estate and then, being unable to pay his debts, sold off the freehold. The purchasers were two brothers-in-law, Beaumont Hotham, later Lord Hotham, and Thomas Sutton, whose descendants are still lords of the manor.

Unlike the manor of Molesey Matham or East Molesey, the West Molesey manor was sold off by the Crown soon after being released from the chase. In 1553 it was granted to Sir Richard Cotton, comptroller of the Royal Household; in 1570 it was acquired by Thomas Brende, a newly rich lawyer, and it stayed with his descendants, passing by marriage to the Smyth family, until Sir Robert Smyth, who achieved some notability as a supporter of the French Revolution, sold it in 1786 to the owners of the East Molesey manor.

Besides these manors, Domesday mentions three other small estates in Molesey, all of which were given to Richard Fitzgilbert, and by him let to two sub-tenants. One of them was just called John, about whom nothing seems to be known, and who leaves nothing to the history of the place. The other was Roger d'Abernon, a knight from the village of Abernon in Normandy. D'Abernon's descendants continued to live at Molesey for the next seventy years or so, before migrating to Stoke, just beyond Cobham. That village, of course, has now added the patronymic to its own name to distinguish it from the dozens of other places also called Stoke throughout England. By the 12th century these three separate holdings were amalgamated into one manor under the hands of the d'Abernon family.

About the year 1130 Engelram d'Abernon, as a deed of piety — what the official citation calls 'for the redemption of the souls of himself, and his brother Jordan, and his father and mother and his lord Gilbert, and for the welfare of the glorious king Henry' — presented the whole manor, lock, stock, and barrel to the Priory of Merton. As the deed proclaimed, this included 'all his land in Moleseya, with all land in plain and wood, and waters and mills pertaining, and free from all service'. Afterwards Engelram stood in the church of the priory 'and granted this gift upon the altar of the Blessed Mary, in the presence of the Prior and all the Convent, and many others both cleric and lay'.

Merton Priory, one of the largest houses of Augustinian friars in England, owned the manor continuously for the next four hundred years, and it thus became known as the *manor of Molesey Prior* or *Molesey Priory*.

In 1518 the great Cardinal Wolsey, who had just completed his magnificent palace just across the river, persuaded the Priory to lease its lands in Molesey to Sir Thomas Heneage, his gentleman usher, for whom he wanted a lodging near at hand. Heneage immediately erected for himself a sumptuous mansion, in which he took up residence. This mansion was probably just off what is now Bridge Road, on the site of Cedar Road. After Henry VIII had taken over Hampton Court and Heneage's eminent master had fallen from grace, the manor was wrested from the hands of the Priory and Sir Thomas became the tenant of the Crown and a servant of the King.

Of the three manors of Molesey, Molesey Prior was the one which stayed longest as Crown property. For about a hundred and thirty years it was let out only on short leases of twenty to thirty years, usually to Royal hangers-on. Then, in 1676 James Clarke, the owner of East Molesey Matham, persuaded the powers to grant him a long lease for 99 years. Soon after that the inhabitants petitioned the King, stating that Clarke, now Sir James, 'has a lease of Molesey Prior for 99 years and has joined it to his own manor of Molesey Matham, by which procedure he encloses the poor tenants common, takes in their landmarks, destroys the King's free chase; therefore praying that the King's manor may not be enclosed to the ruin of the poor inhabitants'. No answer to this entreaty is recorded, and Clarke, a rich and powerful man, apparently continued in the enjoyment of the manor, although it must be said that his successors had to be restrained on occasions when they tried to transfer certain lands from the leasehold manor to the freehold one.

After the expiration of this lease in 1775, the manor was let to a lawyer named Baker John Littlehales, but he soon afterwards sold the remainder of his term to Beaumont Hotham and Thomas Sutton, the joint owners of East Molesey Matham, who obtained renewals of it in 1788 and 1810.

In 1816 George IV, being desirous of purchasing Claremont as a residence for Princess Charlotte, befitting the heir presumptive to the throne, was given permission by an Act of Parliament to sell off enough property to raise a sufficient sum for this purpose. The manor of Molesey Prior was one of the estates in question, and in 1820 the freehold was sold to the lessees. Thus, for the first time since the Saxon era, all the manors of Molesey were under a single ownership, and have stayed so ever since.

Each manor, of course, had a principal house in which the lord lived. That for the manor of Molesey Prior was situated just off Walton Road, where School Road is now. When the manor was in joint ownership with Molesey Matham, it became a farmhouse but, by the middle of the last century, it had degenerated into three very poor tenements. In 1873 it was in such an insanitary state that the medical officer of health reported that 13 persons slept in two rooms, each 13ft by 9ft by 6ft. The house was also totally unfit for habitation — there was no water supply, no water closet accommodation, and near to the house was a pond of filthy and offensive water into which vegetable matter and refuse were thrown. The report continues with a statement which is perhaps the most puzzling to modern ears: 'The only redeeming part about the house is that it has no windows'. It was swept away a few months later.

The East Molesey Matham manor house is the only one still standing, as No 6 Matham Road. At one time it was much larger than it is now. What remains is mostly 18th century, although some experts think that parts may date back as far as the 14th. Internally it has secret passages, a hiding hole, and a good staircase with barley-sugar balusters.

The position of the original manor house for West Molesey Matham is unknown, but it is possible that it was a house which stood in High Street on the site now occupied by Manor Court housemother scheme for the elderly. This house, a delightful medley of facades and gables, dated back to the time of the first Elizabeth. It was demolished by Esher Council in 1963, a diabolical piece of municipal vandalism.

After the amalgamation of all the manors the lords, when they lived locally, usually occupied either East Molesey Park, or Hurst House in West Molesey. Both are now demolished. The house in Bell Road now called Old Manor House was never a manor house.

Copy of an entry in the Court Books of the Manor of Molesey Matham, relating to a Court Baron held on 24 July 1771.

ABOVE: Manor house of the Manor of Molesey Prior, after it had become a farmhouse. It stood on the western side of what is now School Road, and was demolished in 1875. LEFT: Richard Fox, Bishop of Winchester in the reign of Henry VII, lord of the manor of Molesey Matham. RIGHT: Bookplate of Sir Robert Smyth, lord of the manor of Molesey Matham or West Molesey in the 18th century.

2 Guineas Reward.

WHEREAS, some Person or Persons have frequently within the last Fortnight, broken down and stolen the RAILS and FENCES of certain Inclosures on Dunstable Common, in the occupation of Mr. CHARLES BATES.--And Whereas, about a Fortnight ago, a COPPER with a large Cock affixed to it, the Property of the said Mr. Charles Bates, but remaining in an Out-house, on the Farm, belonging to Mr. TODD, at Molesey, was stolen and carried away by some Person or Persons unknown.

NOTICE is therefore hereby given, that the above Reward of TWO GUINEAS will be paid on Conviction to any Person or Persons who will give such information as may lead to the apprehension of the Person or Persons Guilty of either of the above Offences, by the "Association for prosecuting Persons who shall commit Felonies, &c. within the Hundreds of Kingston and Elmbridge and Parish of Chessington in the County of Surrey".

WILLIAM WALTER,
Solicitor to the said Association.

KINGSTON, February 12th 1821

J. Fricker, Printer, Kingston.

Tudor Times

'Why come ye not to Court?
To which Court?
To the King's court,
Or to Hampton Court?'
                                John Skelton (d1529)

From the moment in 1514 when the ambitious Wolsey determined on the construction of his showpiece palace, right on Molesey's doorstep, it was inevitable that its effect upon the neighbouring area would be considerable. At the start, experienced artisans and unskilled labourers would be required for the building work, many of whom were recruited locally, including, as the records show, stonemasons John and William Reynolds of Molesey.

When the wily Cardinal made his fruitless gesture to hand the Palace over to the King, to become Henry's favourite residence, things hotted up apace. Property was eagerly sought in the area by officers of the household, and courtiers of every description who craved a *pied-a-terre* within easy call of their regal master. Even the ferryman, catering for the toing and froing across the river, reaped a rich harvest.

The road system of the district altered radically when Henry acquired Oatlands, and a new thoroughfare, the present Hurst Road, was cut across Molesey's fields to provide a direct communication between the two palaces, eliminating the tedious indirect route through our two villages. Thus Molesey had one of the first by-pass roads ever to be constructed in the Kingdom.

Not that things always worked to the advantage of the locals — far from it. Having an autocratic Tudor sovereign as a near neighbour had decided drawbacks, and was to have a devastating effect on Molesey.

Henry's greatest delight was to be found in the sports of the field — stag hunting, coursing, hawking, and so on. For these purposes, Windsor Park and the hare warrens of Hampton were kept well stocked. By 1535, however, the King was growing middle aged, his weight was vast, his legs were swollen and ulcerated, he was often wracked with pain, and he could no longer bear the journey to Windsor. So, if His Majesty could not go to the sport — the sport must come to him. A huge hunting park like Windsor was to be built around Hampton Court.

OPPOSITE ABOVE: Old Manor House, West Molesey, demolished in 1963. BELOW: Handbill for apprehending a criminal, 1821.

No sooner was the design conceived than its execution was put in hand. Henry secured Acts from Parliament enabling him to acquire all the lands the project required, including the Molesey manors and certain other property, which he exchanged with their owners for ex-monastic lands elsewhere. The Hampton Court Chase, as the park was called, stretched as far as Weybridge and Byfleet. It was specifically reserved for the 'nourishing, generation, and feeding of beasts of venery, and fowls of warren' for the King's sport and pleasure. To retain the deer and game within the park and to exclude marauding poachers it was necessary that the chase should have a high fence all around it. A grant, therefore, was made of £600 for 'paling, ditching, and quicksetting' of the same.

It was provided in the Act that all the same 'liberties, jurisdictions, privileges, and laws, and officers necessary for the punishment of offenders that appertain to any ancient forest in the kingdom, should also belong to this', and forest laws were harsh.

Although the rights of the residents were technically safeguarded by the Act, the new conditions caused great distress. Crops were so seriously damaged by deer that land was left uncultivated, people left the district, and houses were allowed to fall into ruin. The King in his old age was a dangerous man against whom to raise complaints, but by 1545 'certayne men of Molsay and other townes in the chase besides Hampton Court' were driven by desperation to complain of their sufferings to the Privy Council. No redress, however, was offered while Old Harry was alive, but as soon as he was dead and the boy-king Edward VI was on the throne, a further petition was launched.

This new request was brought by 'many pore men of the parishes of Walton, Waybridge, Est Molsey, West Molsey, Essher, Cobeham, and Temsditton', stating 'That by reason of ye making the late chase of Hampton Court, Forasmuch as their Comons, Meadows, and Pastures be taken in, and that all the same parishes are over laide with the Deere now increasing daily upon them, very many households be let fall down, ye families decayed and the King's liege people much diminished, the country there about in manner made desolate, over and besides that, that the King's majesty loseth yearly, diminished of his yearly revenues and rents to a great sum'. This time a commission of enquiry was set up, which recommended the disparking of the chase and the removal of the deer to Windsor, which seems to have been advised, less on grounds to relieve local distress, than on the financial loss and the enormous cost of replacing the park fence which was fast falling down.

After this recommendation had been put in hand, the villages reverted more or less to their old life again.

ABOVE: Hampton Court Palace from the Molesey bank. The building of the Palace had a great effect on the development of the district. LEFT: Cardinal Wolsey, creator of the Palace. RIGHT: Parish pump, West Molesey, removed c1930.

ABOVE: Hampton Court station soon after its opening in 1849; East Molesey Mill is on the left and the Castle Hotel and the bridge on the right. BELOW: Walton Road, East Molesey, in 1863, looking towards the New Inn; the barns of Manor Farm are on the left, and the stream flowing to Cassey Bridge, with the spire of the old parish church peeping over the meadow, to the right.

Into Suburbia

'Ye who from London's smoke and turmoil fly,
To seek a purer air and brighter sky'.
                John Heneage Jesse (1815-1874)

When the author penned these lines he may well have had local residents in mind; he knew the area well, for he was himself the son of the naturalist and writer Edward Jesse, who lived at one time at West Molesey.

The Molesey that Jesse knew enjoyed a peaceful agrarian existence, the two villages combined nourishing less than a thousand souls. In fact, one writer in 1844, after rambling along the river Mole, extols the scene thus: 'near its termination we pass through the pretty rustic village of East Moulsey'. Two years later, however, an Act passed through Parliament, the effect of which (although it was perhaps not appreciated at the time) was for ever to shatter Molesey's pastoral tranquillity. This devasting piece of legislation was innocently entitled *An Act to enable the London and South-western Railway Company to make a Branch Railway to Hampton Court Bridge in the County of Surrey*.

The most crucial date in the whole of Molesey's history was arguably 2 February 1849, for on that date Hampton Court station was opened which, besides bringing more and more daily visitors, precipitated Molesey into commuterdom. Before this, a few wealthy people had enjoyed the privilege of working in London and living comfortably in the country, but these were mostly either court or political office holders or rich merchants. Now the benefits of both worlds could be shared by some of the slightly less well off.

In an instant the fields and meadows, market gardens and groves, were eligible sites for desirable villas, and local landowners were not slow to recognise the golden potential of the asset on which they sat.

The most successful of these was a Hampton lawyer and property developer named Francis Jackson Kent who, even before the railway line was opened, visualised the enormous possibilities for profit the land possessed. As early as March 1848 we find him negotiating the purchase of plots of land in East Molesey. By the end of 1850 he was the owner of all the land bounded by the river Thames, Hurst Lane, Walton Road, and Bridge Road, with the exception of that south of Keen's Alley, which was owned by the Arnison family and others, and the small Feltham estate near the lock. In all this comprised some 300 acres, for which he paid something like £60 to £80 an acre. Kent immediately set about laying down roads across the estate, which was eponymously named Kent Town — a name which even the Ordnance Survey adopted. Building plots were offered for sale along the roads, some of which realised over £4,000 an acre — quite an appreciation over his initial outlay.

The land nearest to the station was quite naturally the centre of Kent's earliest sales. Here, firstly in Palace Road and then in Wolsey Road, large mansions were built, mostly with grand family rooms on the main and first floors, and quarters for the servants in basement and attics. Some were even complete with separate stables and coachhouses. For these were the homes only of the rich commuters, whose occupations — gleaned from the census returns — were mainly as high grade civil servants or City merchants. To maintain the exclusivity of this area gates were positioned across the road at the entrance, which a porter was employed to open and close when required. His lodge still stands as No 1 Palace Road.

However, it was obvious that the presence of this community would bring work for others: tradespeople, builders, gardeners, and so on, all of whom would need homes, as would, too, less well off commuters — clerks and the like. In December 1850, therefore, Kent sold off some 50 acres in the south-west corner of his property (in other words as far away from the gentry as he could get it) to an organisation called the Westminster Freehold Land Society, for £4,700.

Now freehold land societies have an interesting history, originating in the political struggles of the disfranchised lower middle classes in the mid-19th century. The right to vote in parliamentary elections had for centuries been limited only to men who owned freehold property worth at least two pounds a year — the 'forty shilling freeholders' — although this had been extended to certain copyholders and leaseholders by the Reform Act of 1832. This property requirement tended, of course, to favour the Tory Party. The Liberals, therefore, promoted the freehold societies with the expressed intention of encouraging the emerging middle classes, mostly tradespeople and small business owners, who would be expected to vote Liberal, to qualify for the franchise by easing the path to property acquisition. The society bought the land, laid out the roads, arranged for the building of houses, and then loaned the money to their members for the intended purchase. By the enterprise in East Molesey, the promoters hoped to gain some 250 votes for the cause — which one Conservative newspaper thundered 'smacks of communism'. The passing of the second Reform Act in 1867 lessened the requirement for land societies, who then dropped their political aims and became the nascent building societies of today.

The laying out of the Molesey property was left to two committee members, Henry Vine and William Pemberton, together with the Society's solicitor, George Edgar Dennes, in honour of whom some of the roads were named (Dennes Road was later corrupted to Dennis Road). The plan projected by these gentlemen contrived some quite fine class distinctions. It would not do in Victorian England, even among Liberals, for citizens with pretensions to mix with the working classes. Therefore, in Vine Road and Kent Road the houses to be built had to contain at least six rooms, have a value of at least £250 each, and have a building line of 25 feet from the pathway; those in Manor, Park, Pemberton, and Dennes Roads, to have at least five rooms, of value at least £150 each, and to be 15 feet from the pathway; those in Hurst Lane were obviously expected to house the lowest class, for here the houses abutted right on to the pathway, and the only restraint recorded was that no pigsty or stable or accumulation of manure or other offensive matter was to be allowed, without first erecting a wall or close fence next to Dennes Road at least six feet in height. These restrictions were clearly relaxed later, probably to allow more dwellings to be accommodated, as indeed was another, which said that no public house or beer shop was to be allowed on any part of the estate, for shortly afterwards the Europa Inn was built.

While all this was going on, the nibbling away of Molesey's fields and orchards was proceeding apace in other areas. Matham Road was laid around the grounds of the old Matham Manor House, which in a much truncated form had by then become a farm house. The houses here were also of high value and — like Palace Road — gates were placed across the entry with a porter and lodge house (No 36 Walton Road, which was still called 'The lodge' until a few years ago). School Road emerged across the rickyard of the old Priory Manor Farm. A market garden stretching from Manor Road to Bridge Road was developed by its owner, John Arnison, and his brother-in-law George Langley Hansler. The plot of land between the lock and the bridge, belonging to James Feltham, also disappeared under bricks and mortar. Shops started to appear in a long straggle all along the main road from Hampton Court downwards. The name of the main road had never properly been defined, different parts being called different things by different people, but in 1868 it was officially named as Bridge Road from the bridge to Esher Road, and Walton Road from there westward.

The resultant influx of population is reflected in the census returns, which show that in the 20 years between 1851 and 1871 the number of people in East Molesey more than trebled — from 765 to 2,409. Such rapid growth could not be accommodated, and was not accommodated, without a certain amount of anguish. The newcomers bore no loyalty to the parish and its past. The original inhabitants resented the way the intruders had been thrust into their little community. In parochial affairs the village split into two factions, which became known as The Old Party and The New Party. Whatever one proposed, the other opposed, and *vice-versa*. Being of more or less equal numbers, things stagnated. Problems were manifested mainly in three particular issues, all of which were aggravated by the very expansion itself, and on which they ought to have made common cause — accommodation in the church, burial of the dead, and the provision of schools. In all of these cases the outcome was settled only by the two sides resolving to divide, a poor solution, the effects of which bedevil us even today.

The church problem, after many years of squabbling, was determined only by the creation of two parishes, each with their own church — St Mary's and St Paul's — which means we are saddled today with two expensive churches to maintain, where one would suffice. The same solution evolved as far as schools were concerned. Everybody agreed that schools were necessary, but would not agree on joint action to provide them. Again each side built their own, and at the same time: St Mary's in School Road, and St Paul's in Park Road. Both opened in 1860. It was not until 1877 that the two schools undertook to unite, with one used for boys and the other for girls and infants, and then only because lack of funds threatened to close St Paul's. Only recently has the necessity of maintaining the fabric of two separate buildings and two separate sites been overcome by the erection of a new school — St Lawrence — in a more delightful location.

It was, however, the last of the three — the provision for burials — that caused the biggest furore. By 1860 the small graveyard around the old church became full up, and an Order in Council was promulgated prohibiting any further interments. It had been realised for some time that this would happen but, because the two factions would not compromise, every attempt to provide a replacement was frustrated. For a time, surrounding parishes accepted bodies for burial in their own churchyards (in fact for two years there were more East Molesey people buried in West Molesey than there were locals), but soon these places said no. Their own graveyards, too, were becoming exhausted. The matter came to a head in 1863, when the three-month-old child of a poor man living in Bell Road died. The baby could not be buried in either East Molesey or West Molesey, so he applied to Thames Ditton and was refused; Esher said they would accept the burial for a fee of three guineas, which the father just could not afford. Still less could he manage to have the funeral at Brookwood Necropolis, the only cemetery available. What was he to do? He did the only thing possible in the circumstance — he buried the infant in the *backgarden of his own house*. This scandal and the uproar it caused jolted the parochial authorities to take action. Mind you, they still took over two years to do so. Eventually they settled on the purchase of a piece of ground in West Molesey, which was still only accomplished by the usual formula of division and demarcation. The plot had to be severed in two, and there were two burial boards, two clerks, and two sets of accounts to be rendered, one for each of the parishes. What a carry on!

Meanwhile the deadly march of relentless development progressed along the road towards West Molesey. In 1876 East Molesey Park, whose grounds ran from the river Mole to Walton Road and from Bell Road to the Europa, came onto the market by the death of the Dowager Lady Clinton. The old house was demolished, and villa residences laid all over the beautiful landscaped park. Lady Clinton lived in Molesey for just 25 years, but has left a legacy making sure that her stay will be a long remembered one, in the names used for the roads on the estate. Her first husband was Lord Clinton, after whose death she married Sir Horace Beauchamp Seymour, and her step-daughter was the Countess Spencer (an ancestress of the Princess of Wales). Furthermore her maiden name was Poyntz, from which the nearby public house was named.

Plans were passed in 1879 for Avern Road, and shortly afterwards Spreighton Road (originally spelled Spreyton, after a village in Devonshire from which the developer came); Langton Road and Grange Road followed around the turn of the century, almost joining the two villages together.

The fields beyond West Molesey village, together with Molesey Hurst Golf Course, disappeared in the 1930s. There had been five farms in the parish. Manor Farm had its farmhouse and yard in High Street, where Cannon Way now is. Its cultivated lands were further away on part of the Hurst and what later became the golf course. Island Farm occupied the land between the rivers Mole and Ember, most of which is now covered by the Island Barn reservoir. The farmhouse was at the corner of High Street and Priory Lane. Church Farm, the 18th century farmhouse of which still survives, lies between Walton and Hurst Roads. The John Nightingale School and the doomed Bishop Fox School now occupy the site, but what its future will be who can tell? Upper Farm stood on land to the south of Walton Road, opposite Church Farm. A small farm called Summers Farm occupied land now part of the Down Street estate, and originally part of Dunstable Common. This was low-lying and often waterlogged and unworkable for much of the winter, hence it was known as 'The Summers'. The farmhouse still stands.

Of the building estates which now occupy these acres, by far the most interesting is that built over Upper Farm, and called 'Howard Houses'. In 1933 an enterprising young estate agent — Donald Gordon Howard — then but 22 years old, conceived the idea of erecting houses inexpensively, in the new cult, a modern unfussy clean-cut style, with flat roofs, plain white walls, and steel-framed windows. The dwellings were constructed so cheaply that, even selling at a price of £395, with repayments of only 9s 9d a week, Howard anticipated making a clear profit of £100 on each. But even after a high-powered advertising campaign, proclaiming amongst other things 'a Suntrap Home on a sunlit estate in a neighbourhood visited for centuries as a show place and a beauty spot', and a huge painted display board on Waterloo station depicting the houses with Hampton Court Palace as a backdrop; even with refunded fares and a fast car from the station; even with an organised river trip from London to West Molesey; and even at this extraordinarily low price, after two years, when 320 houses had been built, only 100 had been sold. Inevitably Howard ended up bankrupt, but later carried on the development as the manager of a firm owned by his wife.

While all these bricks were being laid, the great innovations of the age gradually became available to the residents of Molesey — gas in 1851; piped water in 1871; a fire brigade in 1872; sewerage in 1894; the telephone in 1900, and electricity in 1904. Other activities, sports and social, also followed: a boat club, and three separate annual regattas; football clubs; cricket clubs; a hockey club; a women's hockey club (the first ever to be established anywhere);

Oddfellows; Foresters; a horticultural society; a building society in 1852; a cooperative society in 1872; a working men's club in 1885; a bank (Ashby's, later Barclay's) in 1889, and a cottage hospital in 1890.

We started with a quotation from 1844, describing Molesey as a 'pretty rustic village', and we end with another from 1910 which says 'East Molesey is an ugly suburban looking village'. In 66 years the despoliation was complete.

ABOVE: Motcombe, Palace Road (now demolished); a good example of the mansions erected in the 1850s in the this part of Molesey. BELOW: Walton Road in the flood of November 1894, before the houses and shops on the south side of the road had been built.

31

ABOVE: Hurst Road in flood in 1906. BELOW: Benn's Cottage — formerly standing at the corner of Walton and Kent Roads — demolished 1885.

ABOVE: West Molesey from the air in 1926, before the area was developed. BELOW: Grange Road in flood, probably 1928.

ABOVE: Looking across the river Ember to Esher Road, about the turn of the century. BELOW: Langton Road, built around the turn of the century. OPPOSITE ABOVE: Old cottages in Esher Road, demolished early this century. BELOW: Woodbine Cottage, Pemberton Road, about 1880, Mr Ben Thompson, builder, standing by the gate.

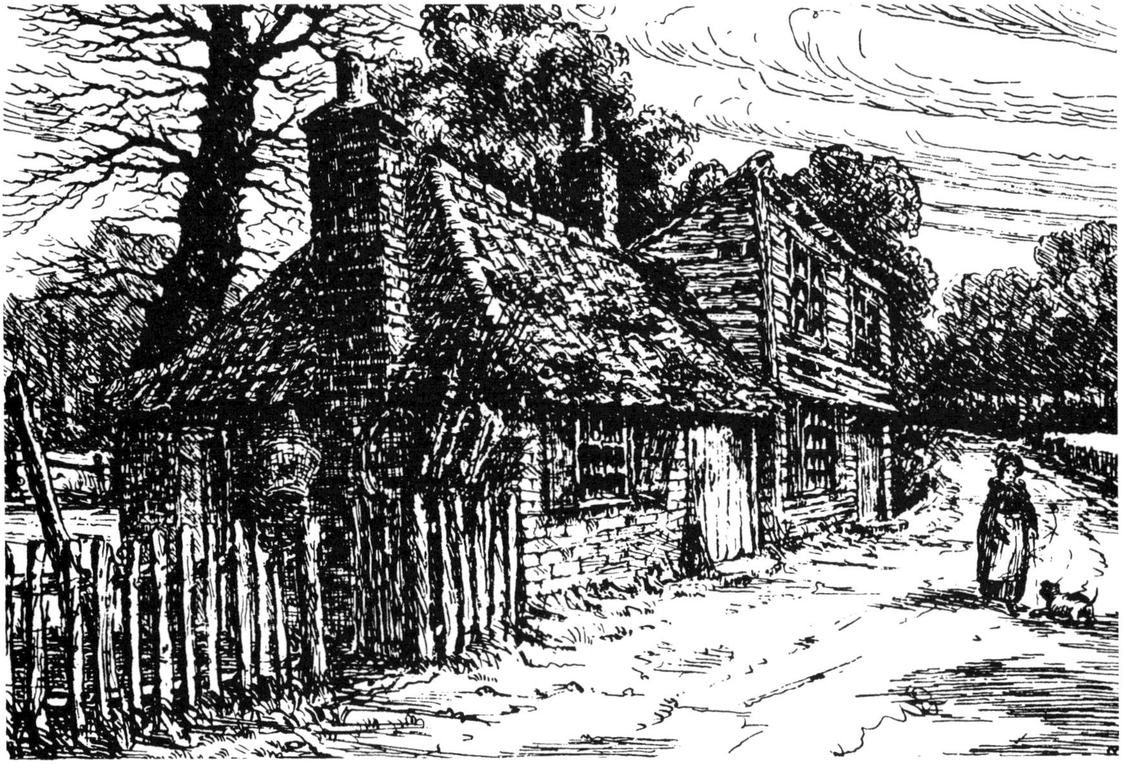

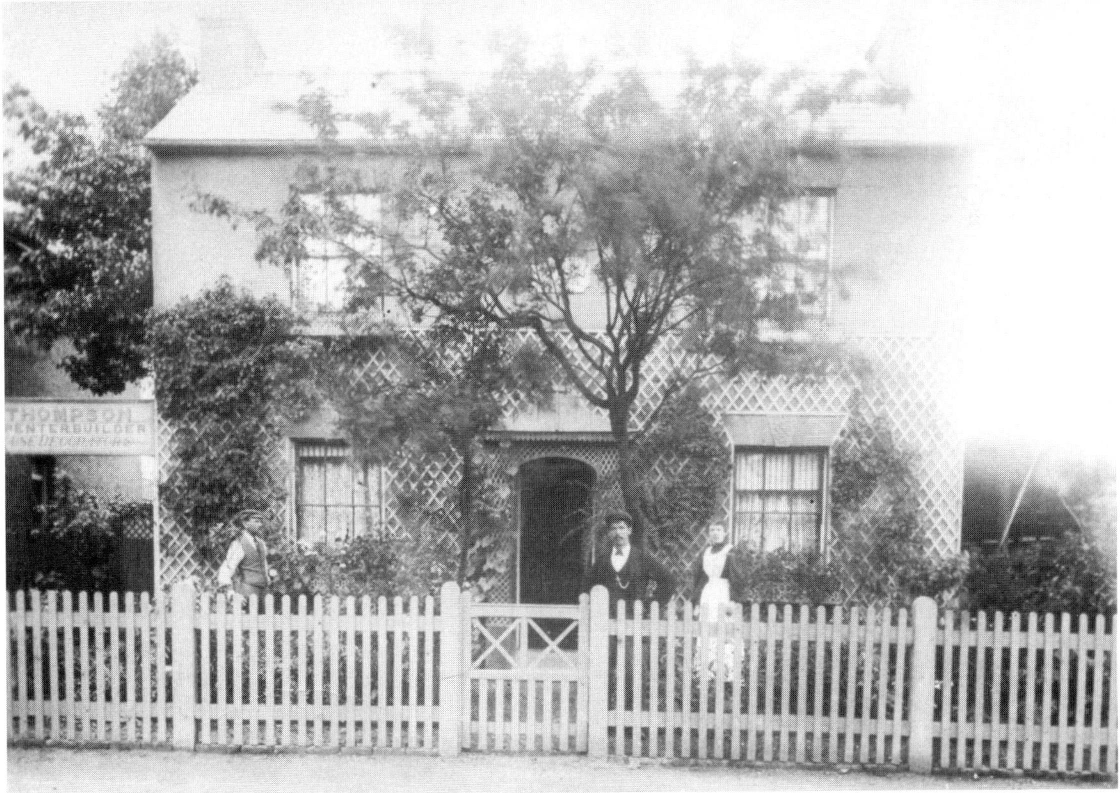
THOMPSON

ABOVE: Esher Road: 1932. BELOW: Meadows on the eastern side of Esher Road in flood, about 1928; Hampton Court Avenue now occupies the site.

ABOVE: Howard Houses in construction, 1934. CENTRE: Advertisement for Howard Houses, 1934. Note the prices! BELOW: Advertisement for houses in Windsor Avenue and Balmoral Crescent.

ABOVE: Municipal housing in Spreighton Road, built 1927, now demolished. BELOW: Bridge Road from the air, about 1948. Note the old Vicarage on the corner of Arnison Road.

ABOVE: Temporary prefabricated bungalows in Tonbridge Road, erected to relieve the housing shortage immediately after the last war, now demolished. BELOW: An 18th century farmhouse — Church Farm.

ABOVE: Island Farm — the farmhouse and barns; CENTRE: the barns; LEFT: the old farmhouse, and RIGHT: Island Barn — now occupied by a reservoir.

ABOVE: St George's Bridge across the river Mole, leading to the Island Barn — rebuilt in iron about 1910, and again in concrete in 1977.
BELOW: Manor Farm, High Street — the entrance to Cannon Way now occupies this site.

ABOVE: Block of 18th century cottages in High Street, now demolished.
BELOW: Aerial view showing how the river Mole originally flowed under East Molesey Mill and into the Thames in front of the station.

ABOVE: Coachman Dunnett negotiates Dr Knox's coach through the water splash in Summer Road. BELOW: Creek Road in the flood of 1894; Mr Smelt's antique shop (now an antique market) is on the left, Hampton Court station in the background, and Creek House on the right.

THE ASSOCIATION OF RIPARIAN OWNERS OF THE MOLE.

The following Notice has been issued by the above Association :—

NOTICE.

THIS RIVER (THE MOLE) has been declared private by the Judgment of the COURT OF CHANCERY on the 3RD DAY OF DECEMBER, 1889.

Persons desirous of putting boats on the River for the day may obtain permits, in accordance with the Rules of the Association of the Riparian Owners of the Mole, of the Water Bailiff, who will be found on the river, or by letter from the Hon. Secretary of the Association, Halfway Lodge, Esher.

BY ORDER.

March, 1897.

The following is a copy of Rule 6, passed at a General Meeting of the Association :—

"6.—The Secretary of the Association, subject to the discretion of the Committee, shall, at the request of any Riparian Owner wishing to grant a mooring on his private property to any respectable resident in the district, issue tickets of permission for boating over the Association water on the following terms, viz. :—For annual tickets, one guinea each boat; and for daily tickets, one shilling each boat; but no ticket shall be given by or to any person letting boats for hire without the consent of a General Meeting of the Association."

Warning notice issued concerning the river Mole, after a successful court case in 1897.

ABOVE: Molesey Mechanics Band. LEFT: The old parish school, West Molesey. The large door at the end was inserted during the last war, when the building was used as a fire station. RIGHT: West Molesey school, about 1920.

ABOVE: 2nd Molesey scout group, 1928. BELOW: Wing Cdr Valerie and members of the British Legion outside the clubhouse, about 1925.

ABOVE: West Molesey school netball team, 1921. BELOW: East Molesey St Paul's football team, 1909.

ABOVE: East Molesey St Mary's junior cricket club c1900. BELOW: Molesey Youth Club, at Carnival time, about 1948.

Here is the Church

'Here is the church, and here is the steeple,
Open the door and here are the people'.
Nursery rhyme

Little many other things, it is to Domesday Book that we must turn to find the earliest mention of a church in Molesey. It appears on the holding of Odard Balastarius. Probably the monks of Chertsey Abbey first planted it here for, wherever Benedictines controlled the land, the brethren brought the Cross. No details of the building have survived. It undoubtedly would have been of extremely elementary timber construction, of modest size, and almost certainly on the site of the present St Mary's.

A more solid church of mortar and flint rubble was erected in the 12th century, and survived until the Victorian era. It was still a small edifice, of nave and chancel only, the whole about 52 feet long by 26 feet wide. By 1368 the fabric had fallen into such disrepair that, following a visitation by the Bishop, the Dean was instructed to hold an inquiry to find out who was responsible for its maintenance and to issue directions for its repair. The roof, at first probably thatched but later tiled, was crowned at the western end by a small weather-boarded tower surmounted by a splay-foot spire. On either side of the nave was a family pew, each a small room about ten feet square and entered only from the outside. That on the south side was built in 1712 for Mr Hezekiah Benson of Bridge House, and that on the north, which was divided in two, in 1760 for Captain John Clarke and Charles Carpenter. In each case permission was given to enclose part of the churchyard, and to be forever appropriated to their respective houses.

In 1849 the building was described as 'a pretty rustic structure'. Its pride, however, was the number of monumental memorials to be seen on the inside. Some of these were high baroque ornaments, inscribed with a plethora of fulsome compliments such as the epitaph writers could tax their minds to devise. Most of these are now preserved in the base of the tower of the present church, but lack of space makes their display extremely limited.

The church, being so small, could only seat some 135 people, and for many years was far too small for the population of the village. Although St Paul's had been opened in 1856, pressure on the accommodation continued. Agitations had been afoot since 1843 to rebuild the church, but all attempts had been frustrated by lack of funds and personal animosities.

On Sunday 6 December 1863 the people went to church as usual and, being a cold wintry day, the wardens lit the stove to keep the congregation warm, which they evidently failed to make certain was fully dowsed before they left. The next day smoke was observed issuing from the building, where some pews had been smouldering from the heat of the stove; they immediately burst into flames when the door was opened. Help was called and in a short time the fire was extinguished. However, some damage had been done, particularly to the pews, pulpit, and other fittings. References to this fire usually exaggerate the damage caused. In fact the insurance company's estimate for restoration was less than £160. Its importance, nevertheless, lay in that it forced the parochial authorities to act, and they decided on the demolition of the old church and the construction of a new one on the same site.

The architect chosen to design the new church was Thomas Talbot Bury, a student of Augustus Pugin; he chose the Early English style, using Kentish rag stone. He was also responsible for the parish schools (later the Adult Education Centre) and the vicarage (now demolished). The nave and chancel were consecrated on 17 October 1865, a north aisle and tower and spire were added in 1867, and the south aisle in 1883, for which the architect was Bury's old friend Charles Barry, son of the architect of the Houses of Parliament.

Over the years the original dedication of the old church had been lost and, when the new church was consecrated, the name of St Mary was chosen. However, from documents preserved in the British Library and the Surrey Record Office, it is now clear that in Tudor times St Lawrence was the patron saint.

East Molesey was at one time a part of the parish of Kingston upon Thames, whose vicar appointed a curate to serve the needs of the people, although from early times it enjoyed some parochial privileges. In 1769, under a private Act of Parliament, East Molesey, together with certain other places, was separated from the mother church to form what was called an ecclesiastical district, and the incumbent was entitled perpetual curate. It was not until 1868, when a general Act was passed allowing all benefices to be designated parishes, that the three ministers of Molesey could claim the right to be called vicars.

The coming of the railway in 1849 increased the population of East Molesey rapidly. In 1854 Mr Kent, who had long campaigned to have the parish church moved onto his new estate, decided to escalate the matter by building a church in the middle of his development, and offering it to the village in lieu of the old overcrowded building. This proposal was turned down by the older residents, as it meant moving their sacred edifice away from its time-honoured site to a new one on the edge of the parish. Mr Kent then applied to the Ecclesiastical Commissioners for leave to open it as a district church with himself as patron, and this was granted. The church was opened for divine service on 24 February 1856, and consecrated by the Bishop of Winchester later in that year. It consisted at first of nave and chancel, seating about 250 people. As further accommodation became necessary, a south aisle was added in 1861-2; a north aisle in 1864, and the nave was extended in 1870. In 1887-8 the church was completed by the addition of a tower and lofty spire, with a baptistry beneath, and a total seating capacity of 500. The style is Perpendicular, and the architect was Stephen Salter.

The earliest mention of a separate village of West Molesey was in the latter part of the 12th century, and it is probable that a church was first built here at that time. It was a low building, of nave and chancel only, with a small porch on the south side. The walls were constructed of plastered rubble with some small round flints, and were in some places nearly five feet thick. The roof was probably originally made of thatch, but was later tiled. In the 15th century the present tower was added, and it seems probable that there was an intention then to rebuild the whole church, but the scheme was never put into effect. The west window was most likely inserted in the early 16th century, as it has a pelican, the badge of Bishop Fox who was lord of the manor here in 1511, sculpted at the apex, although time and the English weather has badly eroded the carving.

In 1843, mainly due to the efforts of the Rt Hon John Wilson Croker, a well-known politician and author who lived at The Grove, where he often entertained some famous people, the dilapidated old church was demolished, except for the tower, and rebuilt on the same site. The architect was John Macduff Derick of Oxford, who chose to build in white brick, in a rather poor, imitation-Gothic style. In 1859 it was enlarged by the addition of a north aisle.

The church contains one or two things worthy of note. The font is a good example of 15th century work. The oak pulpit, with a heavy sounding board, is Jacobean, as is the old communion table, which has now been moved to the north aisle and is backed by a screen carved and painted by the late Rev E. A. Sydenham, vicar here in the inter-war years. A piscina saved from the original building is incorporated in the walls of the chancel, and there are several old memorials, including a brass to Thomas Brende, who died in 1598, his two wives and his eighteen children, and a 17th century cryptogram on a black marble tablet to Frances Thorowgood.

Just as happened in East Molesey, over the years the original dedication of the church became forgotten. During Mr Sydenham's incumbency, permission was sought to have the building re-consecrated and, on 3 July 1928, the rather rare service of re-dedication was performed by the Bishop of Guildford and, by the wish of the parishioners, St Peter was elected as its patron saint.

In October 1936 a mission church dedicated to St Francis was opened in Eastcote Avenue, on what was then a rapidly expanding housing estate, to do duty both for religious purposes and as a community hall. A sliding screen was provided to conceal the altar when the building was in secular use. However, the need for separate services in this area soon proved to be unnecessary, and the hall became used almost entirely for social functions. In 1971 the Charity Commissioners sanctioned its demolition and the sale of the land for the erection of a block of flats.

In the early part of the last century, dissenting services were held in various cottages, including one in Bell Road. In 1847 Methodist meetings were held in the classroom of a private school, which a Mr Thomas had opened in Suffolk Cottage, Bridge Road. The school, together with the services, moved to new premises in Tor House, Manor Road, in 1860. The congregation then increased to such proportions that additional accommodation was urgently required. A piece of ground by the side of Tor House was acquired and, mainly by the assistance of Mr Chubb from the well-known firm of locksmiths, a building for about 100 people was erected and opened in 1867, to serve both as meeting hall and Sunday school, until sufficient funds were available to construct a proper church. Enough ground was left in front for the purpose.

Plans were drawn up by Alexander Launder of Barnstaple — a simple edifice in unostentatious Gothic style, of yellow brick with stone dressings. The foundation stones were laid on 3 August 1876, and the first service was celebrated on Whit Sunday the following year. The Sunday school was rebuilt in 1885, unusually consisting of a main hall with 14 classrooms leading from it — allegedly the first institution of its kind. The school was modified and a new community hall constructed in 1970, named Moss Hall, after one of Molesey's pioneer Wesleyans.

As the population of the district increased, so did the number of people who wished to practise non-conforming worship. Many of them trudged all the way to Kingston each Sunday, but by the 1880s there were enough of them to form a congregation locally. A Mr Alfred Hall was chosen as pastor and, under his enthusiastic superintendence, a site was chosen for a church in Bridge Road, which was opened on 14 December 1886. It was soon realised that mistakes had been made. Firstly the scale of the church was much too ambitious for the size of the congregation, so they were loaded with a debt repayment far above their capabilities. Secondly the church was at the wrong end of the village. Membership did not increase and, when the energetic Mr Hall left the district to take up an appointment in Wales, it dwindled even further. Finally the church was closed and sold in November 1896 to Mr Harry Tagg, boat builder, for £1,000, hardly enough to pay off the debts. In the same year a new pastor, Rev George Harper, was appointed and for a time services were held in the Conservative Hall, until enough money was raised to start on a new church. In 1897 that church was begun in Walton Road, almost opposite the end of Park Road. Of corrugated iron on brick foundations, and capable of seating about 250 people, it opened on 15 July 1897. When first built it had an ornamental spire on the front end of the roof, said to be considerably higher than many buildings of its class. The spire was not as secure as it might have been; during a bad storm it was blown right off and ended upside down impaled in the roadway outside. By the early 1930s support had again dwindled. The church was closed and the building was sold to the Molesey Labour Party, who used it as a meeting hall. Just before the last war, together with adjacent property, it was demolished to make way for a parade of shops. The building in Bridge Road still exists, and can best be seen from the little alleyway which leads past Creek Cottages.

Around the turn of the century a community of French nuns, Les Dames de la Mere de Dieu (The Ladies of the Mother of God), founded a convent in a large house called Stonyhurst in Vine Road. In 1905 the sisters gave permission to local members of the Catholic faith to worship in the little chapel they had had erected in the house. It was so popular that it soon proved far too small. Mainly through the energies of the clergy of St Raphael's Church, Kingston, a building of timber and corrugated iron at Putney, where its services were no longer required, was purchased, dismantled, and re-erected on a plot of land adjacent to Stonyhurst. The church, dedicated to St Barnabas, was consecrated and opened by the Bishop of Southwark on 28 November 1906. Seating was for about 120 people.

A fine new church in mottled brick in the Romanesque style, seating some 300 people, was built beside it in 1931. The old building was afterwards used as a meeting hall and school, but was later demolished after being gutted by fire. A new hall now occupies the site.

St Mary's church, about 1900, before extension of the chancel.

ABOVE: East Molesey parish church — 1807. LEFT: East Molesey parish church from NW — 1823. RIGHT: Rev Ebenezer Pelloe, Vicar of St Mary's 1906-1910.

ABOVE: Old Vicarage, Bridge Road, East Molesey, demolished 1857.
BELOW: St Mary's Vicarage, about 1910, stood where Boleyn Court is
now, at the corner of Arnison and Bridge Roads.

ABOVE: West Molesey parish church in the 18th century, and LEFT: in 1823. RIGHT: John Wilson Croker (1780-1857), Privy Councillor, Member of Parliament, Secretary to the Admiralty, and author; the man chiefly responsible for getting West Molesey church rebuilt in 1843.

ABOVE: West Molesey church about 1900, before the building of the lych-gate. The general stores between the church and the Royal Oak was run by William Mason and is advertised as 'The original Tea & Coffee Rooms'. It was taken over in 1910 by Miss Fry, known to all the children who went in for sweets as 'Polly' (although this was not her name). LEFT: St Peter's church from the SW. INSET: Coat of arms of Thomas Brende, d1598, from his brass in West Molesey church. RIGHT: St Peter's Vicarage, before road widening.

ABOVE: St Paul's Church — from a painting, said to have been made by, or for, the architect before the church was constructed, to show how it was intended to look. BELOW: A turn of the century view.

LEFT: Building the spire of St Paul's church, 1888. RIGHT: Princess Frederica, granddaughter of Queen Victoria, who laid the foundation stone of the tower of St Paul's church, on 19 July 1887. BELOW: Choir of St Paul's church, about 1908.

Folk Moot to Borough

'Local Self-Government leads necessarily on, by
its own inherent force, to steady progress'.
J. Toulmin Smith, *Local Self-Government and
Centralisation* (1851)

The machinery of English local government has its roots back in the Anglo-Saxon age and even beyond. A continuous historical thread extends from the folk moots of ancient times through to the borough councils of today. Its earliest form consisted of a grouping together of all the householders in one locality for the mutual maintenance of law and order. Each member pledged to be answerable for the conduct and behaviour of all the others. Probably the group originally consisted of one hundred families, hence the division was known (at least in this part of the country) as a *hundred*. The hundred as an administrative unit is far older than either the county or the parish. That is why some parishes — Thames Ditton for example — extended into more than one hundred.

In the 10th century a Royal ordinance enjoined that a meeting of the men of the hundred was to be held every four weeks, and all were to attend to do justice to their fellows. In those days, of course, there were no palatial town halls in which to meet. The gatherings — originally known as moots but later as hundred courts — were held on some mutually convenient and prominent piece of open territory towards the middle of the district. It was usual for the hundred to be named from the place where the moot gathered. In this district it was by a crossing over the river Mole — then known as the Emele — and was consequently called the *Emely Bridge* or *Elmbridge Hundred*.

Over the years the hundred was gradually superseded by other forms of local administration. Nevertheless, it retained some authority, especially in the realm of justice, right up to the present century, during which it has shed all significance.

During the Middle Ages local government devolved mainly into a manorial function. By the 14th century the lords of both Molesey manors claimed the right to hold a local court — called a *leet* — for the trial of offenders caught within their domain, to search out suspected malefactors who had decamped to other parts and bring them back for trial, and to fine those found guilty and confiscate their goods. All of this was a source of considerable profit. In 1334 it was estimated that the 'perquisites of the courts' of Molesey Matham amounted to six shillings and eight pence a year. They also held separate courts — called courts baron — for the registration of land transactions, for which a charge was also made. The last court baron held in Molesey was as late as 1916.

The manors were also responsible for maintaining and keeping in good order the roads which ran across their land. By early Tudor times, however, the manorial system was in decline. In 1555, to revive the rapidly degenerating highways, the responsibility for their upkeep was transferred to the previously purely ecclesiastical parishes. Each was to appoint a surveyor of the highways, who was to organise their repair and present to the magistrates anyone who caused hindrance.

Thus in 1661 Anne Beckford, a widow living in East Molesey, was accused before the Quarter Sessions at Kingston of allowing a ditch to be so blocked up that it overflowed into the highway. In 1668 Newdon Cole, 'late of West Moulsey', was likewise charged 'that he encroached upon the common highway near the churchyard' for a space of six feet by six feet, which he admitted. He was fined one shilling.

The parish gradually became the most important territorial unit. The system worked through a series of local officers appointed at an annual parish meeting at Easter: churchwardens, surveyor, overseers of the poor, constable, aletaster, and so on. They were unpaid and untrained, and the work was generally unpopular and perfunctorily performed. The meeting was originally held in the church vestry and was thus called the Parish Vestry. In later times they preferred a more convivial atmosphere — in West Molesey of the Royal Oak, and in 18th century East Molesey of the Castle, King's Arms, Swan, and Bell each of which was visited in turn.

The officers recovered the expenses they had laid out by a rate levied on all property owners. To encourage reluctant parishioners to serve, they were allowed to charge for their subsistence while on parochial business. Some did not stint themselves: the churchwarden of West Molesey, going to Kingston in 1797, charged £1 9s 3d for his dinner.

The officers entered their accounts into books, and these volumes, together with the minutes of vestry meetings, form the basis of parochial records. Some records exist for both the Moleseys from the 18th century. They tell a fascinating and human story of the times, and especially of the trials, tribulations, distress, and suffering of ordinary folk, who were forced to apply to the parish to exist.

After the Napoleonic Wars there was great hardship among the poor. Claims upon the poor rate soared, and it was kept down only by administering relief with ever-increasing harshness. In 1822, to reduce costs, the two Molesey parishes established a joint workhouse in what is now known as Old Manor House in Bell Road. Here the paupers, orphans, mental deficients and aged were all lumped together and accommodated more cheaply on a communal basis, and relief was generally denied to any who refused to enter the workhouse.

Even so, the cost of poor relief developed beyond the resources of small parishes like the Moleseys. In 1834 the Poor Law Amendment Act removed the responsibilities from parishes and grouped them together into Poor Law Unions, each with a central poorhouse. The governing body of the union was a Board of Guardians, elected on the basis of one per parish, irrespective of size. The Moleseys were combined into the Kingston Union. Henceforth the local poor were required to apply for assistance at the union workhouse in Coombe Lane, Kingston. This system continued until it was abolished by the Local Government Act of 1929. The Kingston Workhouse was then converted into a general hospital.

The 19th century was dominated by much economic, political, and social change, inevitably posing new problems and producing new solutions in the field of local government. A series of devastating outbreaks of cholera in the 1840s prompted the passing of an act in 1848 which precipitated the preservation of public health into the realm of local government, and for about a hundred years became its foremost function. The act provided for the setting up of local sanitary districts, whose duty it was to oversee and control various insanitary aspects contributing to the spread of disease. The Moleseys came within the jurisdiction of the

Kingston Rural Sanitary Authority, which was virtually the Board of Guardians wearing a different hat.

In 1866, after the population growth of East Molesey had brought much new blood into the village, especially professional and commercial men, all demanding a greater say in the running of local services, the parish applied for and received permission for the setting up of a Local Board. This consisted of a locally elected council having paid officials and staff, combining all the functions of the parish vestry, the rural sanitary authority, and the highway board, in one body. East Molesey was, therefore, the first — and for nearly thirty years the only — part of the Borough of Elmbridge to have its own elected council.

The first meeting was held on 13 September 1866, when Mr Frederick Bedwell of Matham Road was elected chairman; Mr John Cann, a solicitor living in Vine Road, was appointed clerk at a salary of £25 a year and Mr John Bent surveyor and inspector of nuisances, at £20 a year. It was resolved that meetings should be held every month at the Bell Inn, although within a short time Mr Cann reported that he had added a room to his own house, 40 feet by 20 feet, suitable for meetings of the Board, which he offered for their use at a rent of £20 per annum. This was accepted and used for some 20 years.

Mr Cann's clerkship to the Board was on a part-time basis only and he continued in private practice. In 1887 due to the increase of his business Mr Cann asked the Board to find alternative accommodation. It moved to new premises on the corner of Walton and Matham Roads. For the first time the Board had its own accommodation, with offices, vehicle depôt, store, and fire station, all at one location, the site of which is now the Walton Road Garage.

The Board soon became involved in street lighting and highway maintenance. The first report of the surveyor stated that: 'The main road is in a very bad state, and requires immediate repair from one end to the other'. However, the main reason for setting up the board was said to be 'The improvement of the health of the Parish by an improved system of surface drainage', a laudable object indeed, but one which, because of certain traits which bedevilled the board throughout its existence, notably parsimony and eternal petty bickering between the members, was put off and put off, and not finally achieved until almost 30 years had elapsed.

Meanwhile, West Molesey, where the population growth was much slower, continued under the administration of its vestry. Its health was tended by the rural sanitary authority, its roads by the Highway Board, and its school by a school board.

Towards the end of the 19th century local government — which had become immured in a prolific welter of various authorities, boards, unions, *ad hoc* bodies, and so on — was entirely reorganised and rationalised.

In January 1889 the poll for the first popularly elected county councils took place. The candidates for the Molesey Electoral Division — which initially included the parish of Esher (much to the chagrin of the latter) — were Mr John Cann, the clerk of the local board, and Mr J. W. Sumner, a stone mason and builder, of Walton Road. Although not standing as official party candidates, it was well known that Mr Cann, who was elected, was a committee member of the local Conservative Association and that Mr Sumner was the secretary of Molesey Liberal Party — so much for politics in local government being a 20th century innovation.

The success of county councils led in 1894 to a second tier, of district councils. The East Molesey Local Board became the East Molesey Urban District Council, with virtually the same powers as before. West Molesey became a parish with a parish council, inside the Kingston Rural District. Even before the reorganisation, however, East Molesey had tried desperately to embrace its western neighbour into its local board area, mainly because it had at last embarked upon the sewerage disposal scheme and wanted West Molesey to help pay for it. The latter wanted nothing to do with it, resisted tenaciously, and succeeded for some time. Nevertheless, the government eventually succumbed to pressure and, by an Order in Council dated 1 October 1895, forced West Molesey to amalgamate, to form the Urban District of East and West Molesey.

With the extra work this entailed, the Council's premises became woefully inadequate, and in 1902 a large house called Dundee Villa in St Mary's Road, with grounds extending back to Walton Road, was purchased and opened as offices, depôt and yard.

It seems that the average span between major local government reorganisations is about 40 years. The East Molesey Local Board was formed in 1866, in 1894 it became an urban district, in 1933 that united with Esher and the Dittons, Cobham, and Stoke d'Abernon, to form the Esher Urban District, which in turn, in 1974, was merged with Walton and Weybridge into the present Borough of Elmbridge. The next move ought, therefore, to be early next century; one wonders what that will bring forth.

Dundee Villa, St Mary's Road — Molesey Council Offices, 1900 to 1933.
Demolished in 1969.

Parish of East Molesey,

SURREY.

THE "HALE & PLATT'S" CHARITY.

SCHEME FOR MANAGEMENT,

LAID DOWN BY THE

CHARITY COMMISSION,

JULY 8th, 1873.

PRINTED FEBRUARY, 1874.

WILLIAM PAYNE, } Churchwardens.
A. KEELING,

KNAPP, STEAM PRINTER, KINGSTON.

ABOVE: East Molesey Court, which might have become the Council's offices and public recreation ground. LEFT: Title page of a scheme for the management of the Hale and Platts Charity, 1873. RIGHT: Dr John Knox, Medical Officer of Health for Molesey from 1899 to 1932.

LEFT: A page from West Molesey Churchwardens' Accounts Book. RIGHT: Coal and Wine Tax post, on the boundary of West Molesey with Walton-on-Thames. OPPOSITE: Poster announcing the distribution of Ray's Charity, 1949. The Charity was provided under the will of James Ray, for many years Chairman of Molesey Council.

EAST & WEST MOLESEY

RAY'S CHARITY

The above Charity consists of a sum of money to be equally divided, one week before Christmas each year, between six male or female persons of good character and of not less than 50 years of age, who must have resided in East or West Molesey for not less that 5 years.

Forms of application in connection with the distribution of the Charity for the year 1949 can be obtained on application to the undersigned, to whom they should be returned not later that FRIDAY, the 2nd. DECEMBER, 1949.

FREDERICK EDWARDS,
Clerk to the Trustees.

Council Offices,
Esher.
12th. November, 1949.

ABOVE: The Lord Mayor of London opens Island Barn Reservoir, 4 November 1911. LEFT: Electricity substation and workshop in Feltham Avenue, erected here in 1882 as a public hall called The Lyceum; before that it was Holy Trinity Church, New Malden. RIGHT: Police box at West Molesey, with the author's father outside.

For the People

> 'It is obvious that all business purely local
> — all which concerns only a single locality —
> should devolve upon the local authorities'.
> John Stuart Mill
> *On Representative Government* (1861)

The first public utility to bring benefit to Molesey was the supply of gas. The Hampton Court United Gas Company was formed in 1851, with works at Hampton Wick. One of its chief promoters was Francis Jackson Kent, then busily engaged in laying out the Kent Town estate. It was probably due to his influence that the area supplied was extended to include the Moleseys. In 1867, by a special Act of Parliament, the firm was incorporated as the Hampton Court Gas Company, a name it bore until the nationalisation of the gas industry in 1949. The original main crossed the river on Hampton Court Bridge, augmented later by another *via* Tagg's Island. The area was connected to the gas grid in 1970.

Soon after gas came to the district the parish of East Molesey decided to light the streets with it. Lighting Inspectors were elected, but could not at first enforce a rate because they had placed lamps in Matham Road, which was then a private street. For some time these were maintained by voluntary contributions. In 1885 the Local Board, who had taken over responsibility, changed all the lamps to oil burning, because some ratepayers complained of the cost. In 1902 it was decided that the extra brightness of gas was well worth the extra expense, and gas lighting was restored. The lamps were converted to electricity in the early 1930s.

In 1871 Parliament passed an act which enabled the Lambeth Water Company to build reservoirs in West Molesey and, in order to appease residents during the trauma of having their streets ripped apart to lay the mains, the company inserted a clause empowering them to supply the houses in Molesey with piped water. Thereafter the sanitary authorities made by-laws compelling all habitable houses to be connected.

The supply of electrical power was first mooted by the Molesey Urban District Council in 1901, but for some reason no action was taken. It was adopted two years later by a commercial firm — the Twickenham and Teddington Electric Supply Company. By 1904 the cables had been laid and the first houses supplied.

Molesey was coupled to the telephone network on 1 October 1900, in what was then a commercial system operated by the National Telephone Company. The exchange was in a building in Manor Road next to the Poyntz Arms inn. A public call office was established for non-subscribers at 44 Walton Road, now part of Colena Ladies Outfitters, and another soon after in Mr Usher's ironmonger's shop, now Quality Hardware, at 53 Bridge Road. The charge for a call within the Molesey circuit was one penny, and three pence to either Kingston or London. The Molesey exchange, which was later extended to cover the whole of Hampton and Teddington, was transferred to a site on the other side of the river, near Hampton Church.

East Molesey's first post office was in the Bell Inn, and the licensee, Mr Pitcher, was also the postmaster. About 1867 another office was opened in a shop in Bridge Road, near the Albion Inn. The postmistress was a Mrs Taylor, and her husband ran a coal and corn merchant's business in the same shop. In 1906 Bridge House, No 70 Bridge Road, was purchased and adapted as a main post office, by building a new public office stretching from the old house to the pavement, and by altering the building for telegraphs, sorting, rooms for postmen and telegraph boys, and a residence for the postmaster. After this the Bell Inn became a sub-office, called Upper East Molesey Post Office. This was later transferred to Mr Kent's chemist's shop at the corner of Walton and Spencer Roads, and given the grander title of Molesey Park Post Office. In January 1904 a further sub-office was opened at Mr Wallace's draper's shop on the corner of Walton and Seymour Roads, but in a few years this was transferred to Rowe and Stevens, just up the road, in which shop it still exists.

In West Molesey, like East Molesey, the first post office was in the main hostelry — the Royal Oak. About 1864 it was transferred to Grave's baker's shop, which stood appropriately on the spot where the present postal sorting office stands. In 1900 it moved to the grocer's shop on the corner of Walton Road and High Street. In the early 1950s an additional sub-office was opened in Central Parade.

A volunteer fire brigade was formed in 1872, and the East Molesey Local Board voted a small sum of money for the purchase of hoses, standpipes, a lamp, and a hand cart on which to wheel them around. In 1874 a shed in Park Road was rented at £5 per annum to house the apparatus and the words 'FIRE BRIGADE' were painted on the front. After a meeting was told in 1883 that 'at present they had had not a chance in a hundred of putting out a fire', moves were afoot to purchase a steam fire engine. However, no money for this was forthcoming and it was six years before the village had a fire pump, and then it was only a manually operated one. It was horse-drawn and cost £150, and was operated by men, 13 a side, moving their arms up and down. Thus 115 gallons per minute could be thrown to a height of 125 feet. At the same time new uniforms, hoses, and other equipment were purchased at a cost of £317 3s 6d. The vicar and churchwardens of St Paul's presented the Brigade with a bell to summon the volunteers together whenever the alarm was raised.

The fire station was moved, first to the old Local Board offices on the corner of Walton and Matham Roads in 1887, and then in 1900 to a purpose-built station, which is now the headquarters of the St John Ambulance Brigade.

A horse-drawn steam pump was acquired in 1909. The old manual engine, now a museum piece, is still preserved at the Surrey Fire Brigade headquarters at Reigate. There are some, however, who think that, as it was paid for by local people, a home ought to be found for it in this district. On 24 January 1925 a 32 horse power Dennis motor pump with an extending 35 feet escape ladder was purchased at a cost of £800.

Under the Fire Service Act of 1947, control was transferred to the County Council who, in 1961, closed down the Molesey Fire Station.

Under an Order in Council in 1840 the boundaries of the Metropolitan Police were extended to cover the Moleseys, to take over the tasks previously undertaken by unpaid parish constables. A police station was set up at Ferry Road, Long Ditton but, by the 1880s, complaints were voiced that, because of the large area and the distance away of the station, Molesey ought to have its own police station. In 1899 a police box with a telephone was placed at the corner of Walton and New Roads at West Molesey, and in the next year, under a special Act, the land was purchased for the present station.

A nursing home for local people was founded as a private act of charity by the Dowager Lady Barrow, and opened in May 1890 in a house called Waverley Cottage, next to the Methodist Church in Manor Road. On 27 February 1892 a public meeting was held to appoint a committee to take over the running of the home and raising of funds. In October 1894 the home was transferred to 55 Pemberton Road and renamed the East and West Molesey and Hampton Court Cottage Hospital. It had eight beds and one cot. In 1936 the former isolation hospital in High Street, West Molesey, established by the old Molesey Council, but no longer required for that purpose, was sold to the Cottage Hospital for the nominal sum of £1,000, and the Hospital was transferred to these premises. It was run as a voluntary hospital and served by honorary medical staff. Funds were raised by donations, Pound Days, and the Molesey Carnival, which developed out of an annual parade of Friendly Societies and a sports day. In 1948 the Hospital was merged with the National Health Service.

In Victorian times a small free library was run by the Parish of St Mary. in 1880 this was extended with some 500 volumes donated by Mr Samuel Carter Hall, a well-known author and local resident, to cover the whole village. The books were issued from the Girls' School, at the rate of about 60 a week. In 1926 the District Council was pressed to enter the county library scheme, which had been adopted by Surrey the previous year, but they refused, sinced it meant raising a rate of a penny in the pound! In 1927, however, they relented, and eventually a hut was erected in the council grounds at Dundee Villa, St Mary's Road. This was used until the present library was opened in 1964.

The Bell Inn — East Molesey's first post office.

ABOVE: East Molesey Fire Brigade outside their fire station at the corner of Walton and Matham Roads. BELOW: Lt F. Hodge (Capt) and members of the Fire Brigade, OPPOSITE ABOVE: with the steam pump purchased in 1909. BELOW: Capt A. Angus, second officer D. Higgins, and the Brigade pose outside the fire station with the Dennis motor pump acquired in 1925. Mr Alfred Lincoln appears on this photo, on that with the steam pump, and also on that with the manual pump in 1897.

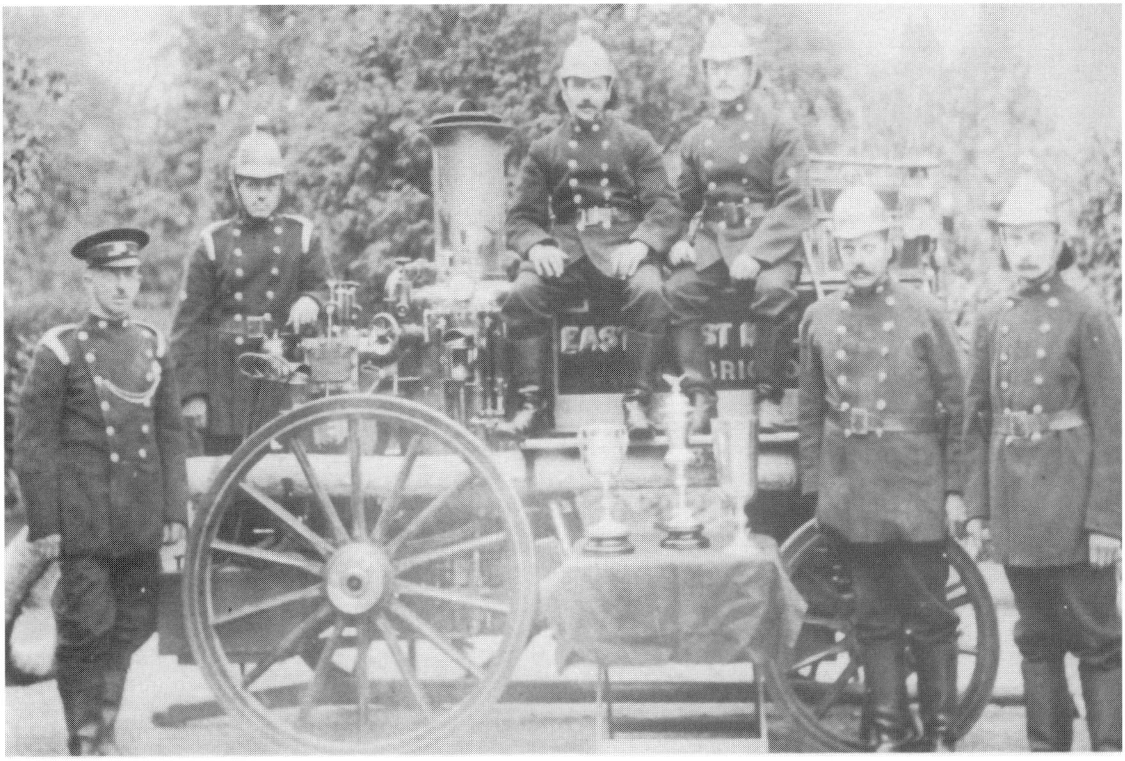
EAST

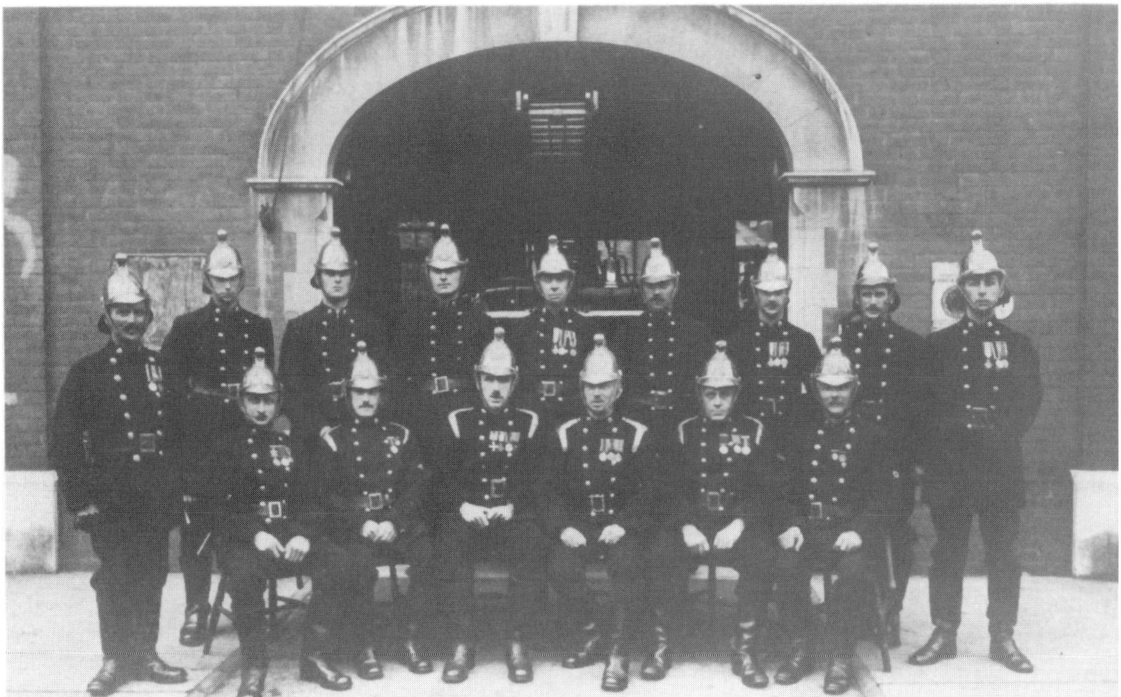

ABOVE: East Molesey Police station, opened in 1901. LEFT: Molesey policemen getting to duty during the floods of 1929. RIGHT: Molesey Cottage hospital in Pemberton Road, destroyed by a flying bomb on 8 August 1944.

ABOVE: Bridge Road in the flood of November 1894. BELOW: The Jubilee Fountain in Bridge Road, Creek House in the background, about 1910.

ABOVE: West Molesey's war memorial in its original position at the corner of Walton Road and New Road. BELOW: The Mole bridge in Esher Road before the building of the footbridge.

ABOVE: Aerial view, about 1948: Arnison Road, Grove Road, the old Girls' School, and the Methodist church may be picked out. BELOW: The footbridge in Summer Road, now disappeared under the flood prevention scheme.

ABOVE: Hampton Court bridge, about 1920, showing the old outfall of the river Mole, and the bridges which had to be crossed to get to the station. BELOW: St Andrew's Hall, built in 1900 by Rev Henry Hollingworth, and sometime used as an infants' school; now the Royal British Legion Club. OPPOSITE ABOVE: Teachers and pupils of West Molesey school in Victorian days. BELOW: Mr B. J. Bonar and pupils of East Molesey Boys' School, 1905.

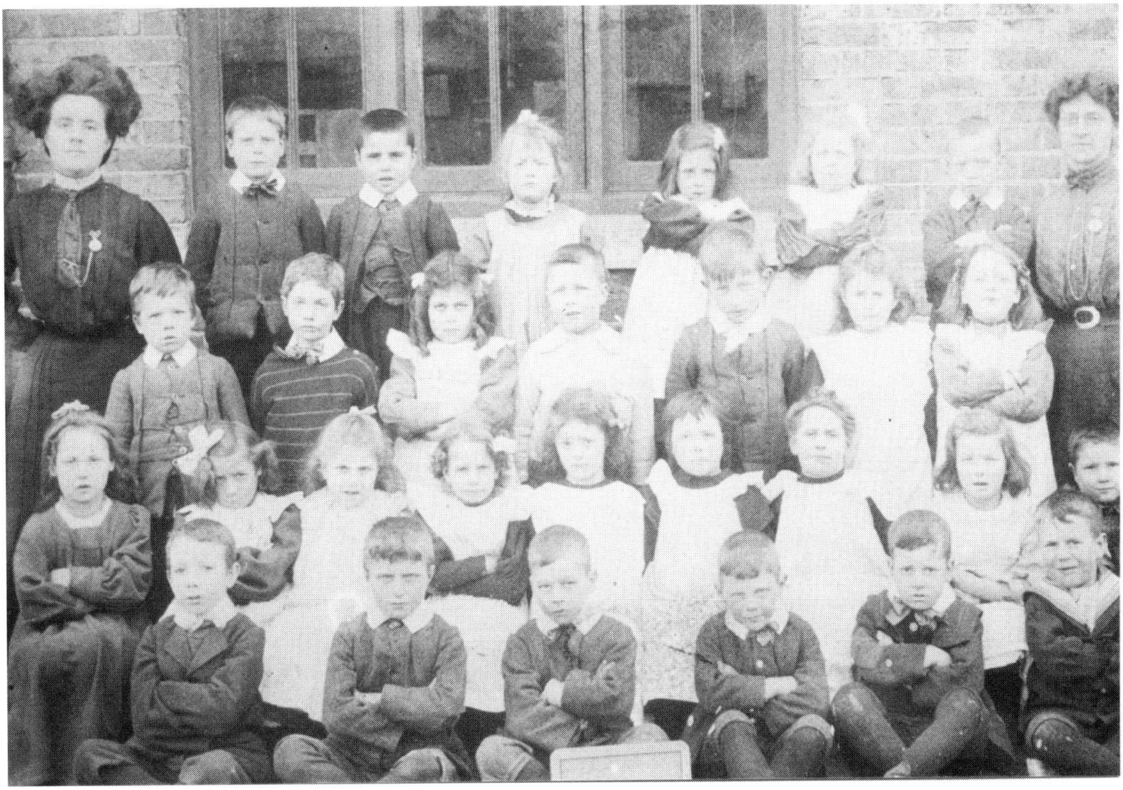

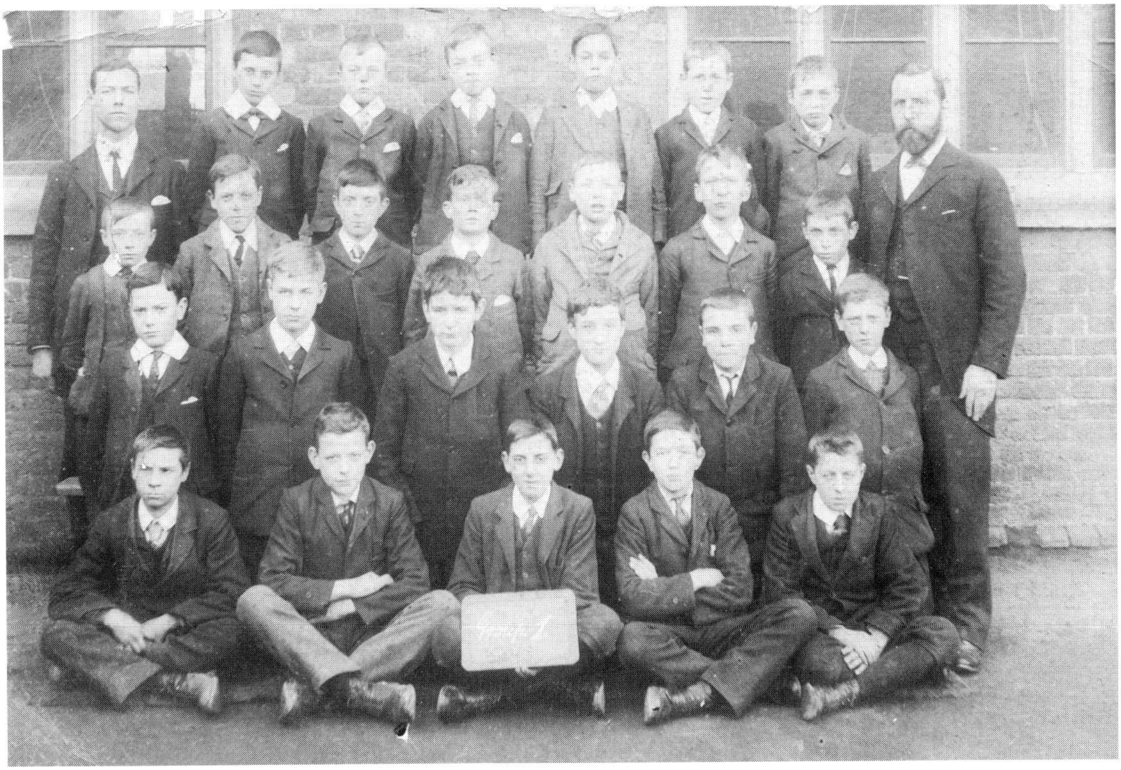

LEFT: East Molesey Park, about 1850, built by the side of Upper Mill.
BELOW: East Molesey Mill about 1894. This part of the river Mole, known as 'The Creek', is now filled in. RIGHT: The Mill showing the landing stage from which barges were loaded and unloaded with corn and timber.

Honest Toil

> 'The finest gentry it has ever been my good fortune to meet have been the craftsmen, blacksmiths wheelwrights, shepherds, slatters, saddlers and millers. It is sad to think that they are on the decline'.
>
> S. P. B. Mais, *Our Village Today* (1956)

From the start of its history right through to the beginning of our century, Molesey saw little of what we today usually term 'industry'. The staple employment of Molesey's sons (and many of its daughters too) lay in the field of agriculture, or of related pursuits. The villagers were practically self-supporting: the blacksmith repaired the ploughs and shod the horses; the miller ground the corn and the baker baked the bread; the innkeeper brewed his own beer; the wheelwright, the carpenter, the tailor were all local craftsmen. It was not until late in the day that shopkeepers appeared on the Molesey scene, and not till very late that the commuter's requirements brought the Victorian 'emporium', and the 20th century, the supermarket.

The rich alluvial soil on which Molesey stands is extremely fertile, unlike that of some of our near neighbours, which have large tracts of dry acid unproductive ground, not worth the trouble of enclosing and so left as the commons we see today. Molesey has no such commons. Even the small area known as 'Cow Common' is not, strictly speaking, common land.

Under the manorial system the land was cultivated on a communal basis. The arable area was divided into three huge open fields, several dozens of acres in extent, in which each tenant held a number of strips, each one furlong (220 yards) in length and one pole (5¼ yards) wide, scattered throughout the field. A number of strips were known in Molesey as either a shot or a furlong, each having a separate and distinctive name, most of which are now lost. But the following are representative of those which have survived: Lydmore Shot, Polfurlong, Stanfurlong, and Le Fullack.

As far as East Molesey is concerned the open field system seems to have died away quite early, probably during Tudor times when it was Crown land, and the area was divided into smaller compact units called closes. But in West Molesey the common field system continued until 1821. These fields were Churchfield, which ran between Walton and Hurst Roads, from the parish church to the Walton boundary; Crossfield, which was on the eastern side of the village, across both sides of Walton Road, and Crabstile Field, which covered the land lying between High Street and the river Mole, south of Walton Road.

Surrounding the arable fields, and bordering the rivers, were the lush green meadowlands, which were also sub-divided among the tenants and farmed in common. Hay was grown on the meadows in spring, but it all had to be mown, dried and gathered before Lammas Day (1 August), and from then until Candlemas Day (2 February) they were thrown open for the grazing of cattle. The meadows in Molesey were: The Hurst, which lay entirely in West Moseley, on both sides of Hurst Road; two separate meadows both called Lot Mead, one in West Molesey and one in East, and so called because each man's holding was allocated by drawing lots; East Molesey Common, which stretched alongside the southern bank of the Mole from what is now the Nielson Playing Field to Hampton Court; and Dunstable Common, which was on the north side of the Mole in West Molesey between Green Lane and High Street. The commoners' beasts could also browse on the stubble of the arable fields after the crops had been harvested, and on the fallow field for the whole year. In fact, it was the droppings of the animals running the land which replaced the nitrogen in the soil and allowed the system to continue.

By the beginning of the 19th century, the shortcomings of this archaic system were increasingly obvious. On 25 November 1814 a petition from the main landowners in Molesey was presented to the House of Commons, seeking permission to bring in a private Bill to rearrange the land. The Bill was passed, and received Royal Assent in the following July as 'An Act for Inclosing Lands in the Parishes of East Molesey and West Molesey, in the County of Surrey'.

Under the Act, each man's holdings were re-allocated in single compact units, and from 1821 the landscape of the two parishes took on a new face. Fences and hedges sprang up around the new enclosures, trees were planted, and new farm houses built, setting the pattern of fields, hedgerows, roads and farms, which stamp their mark on the map of Molesey even today, though most of them have long been built over.

At the same time the Act extinguished the tithes which farmers had to pay, and the owners received awards of land in lieu. The lords of the manors, as lay rectors of the great tithes of East Molesey, received large pieces of East Molesey Common, for the grant of which they were charged with the liability of maintaining the chancel of the parish church. The owners of this land, currently the Trafalgar House Group, still have this obligation.

From that time the agriculture of Molesey, particularly of East Molesey, veered away from traditional cereal crops towards market gardening and fruit growing. Such produce found a ready sale among the sprawling masses of London, until these acres themselves were swallowed by the ever-voracious appetite of that same Great Wen.

In early manorial times, each lord of the manor provided a mill to which all his tenants were perforce obliged to take their corn. There were in Molesey three mills, powered by the waters of the Mole and Ember; we should more strictly speaking say that there were two and a half, because Ember Mill, the mill of the manor of Ember or Imber, sat astride the river and was half in East Molesey and half in Thames Ditton. The other two both stood on the river Mole.

The mill of the manor of Molesey Matham, known as Upper Mill, stood on what is now part of the sports ground of the Standard Chartered Bank; and the Lower Mill, or Sterte Mill, that of the manor of Molesey Prior, still stands not far from Hampton Court Station.

In the early 13th century antagonism between the two mill owners burst into open conflict. The owner of the lower mill, the Prior of Merton, complained that the owner of the upper mill, Sampson de Molesey, had diverted the course of the river, thereby depriving him of essential water. Furthermore, when he sent his men upstream to reinstate the former course of the river, Sampson took away their picks and shovels by force of arms and prevented them from completing their task. The Prior then appealed to King John, who personally ordered a jury to sit and decide the matter. Their verdict is a lengthy document, detailing what each side should do at the various places along the river. Today it is virtually impossible to identify with any degree of certainty the names and locations mentioned.

During the Commonwealth both mills were acquired by a man named John Samine, and for a time embarked upon a real industrial career — the manufacture of gunpowder. However, as soon as the monarchy had been restored, thirteen residents of East Molesey petitioned the new King: 'humbly beseeching your princely goodness to order that the said mills may be taken away or removed to such distance from the said Town that your petitioners may quietly enjoy their habitation and not be left in such perpetual fear and terror', carefully pointing out that one of the mills was directly opposite the King's own house at Hampton Court. It is perhaps significant that, shortly after this, Lower Mill ceased making gunpowder and reverted to the grinding of corn, while Upper Mill carried on its deadly trade for another hundred years.

That the fears of the residents were in some ways justified is proven by a number of serious and often fatal accidents. As early as 1669 the store caught fire and Samine lost powder to the value of £1,200, as well as £660 worth of powder belonging to the King, for which he was responsible. In 1706 an explosion killed Thomas King, a labourer working at the mill; and in 1771 the burial register of East Molesey records 'Francis Weasen and Thomas Hawkins distroyed by ye gunpowder Mill'. The worst disaster, however, seems to have been in 1754, when *The Gentleman's Magazine* reported: 'Saturday, October 19th. About two in the afternoon, a place called the Dust-house belonging to Mr. Norman's gunpowder mill at Moulsey, in Surrey, blew up, and killed one man who was barelling up the gunpowder. 'Tis reckoned that there were about 30 barrels of powder in the storeroom each barrel containing about 100 pounds weight [about one and half tons]. The building was blown into a thousand pieces, the poor man's body was blown limb from limb, seven or eight elms torn up by the roots, and the adjacent buildings terribly shaken. Another store-house had the roof blown in, and a man at work received a light blow on the back of his neck by a piece of timber, but the powder remained safe. The houses for many miles about were shaken by the explosion, particularly Hampton Court Palace, and the Speaker's house [Ember Court]. At Croydon it was thought to be the shock of an earthquake'.

About the year 1780 the owners of the powder mills acquired the lordships of the manors and, wishing to set themselves up in style, closed down and demolished all the mill buildings and turned the old mansion alongside, together with all its grounds, into a country estate.

It is difficult to assess just how many men were employed in the gunpowder works. Probably it was never very many. It was dangerous toil, and the employees were ever engrimed by the thick black powder. Locals would almost certainly have shunned it unless the wages were a lot better than those paid in agriculture.

Lower Mill, continuing to grind corn, was rebuilt in 1828, and was described in 1844 as a large, factory-like and most unpicturesque mill. By this time the owner had decided to extend his business to include sawmilling, and an additional structure had been added at one side.

In 1913, after an abortive attempt to use the mill as a cocoa factory, a lease was granted to the Zenith Motor Company for the manufacture of motor 'cycles. The Zenith company had started in small premises in Weybridge encouraged by the proximity of Brooklands Track, and its success was due in no small measure to the brilliance of designer Fred Barnes, who produced one of the earliest spring-framed motor 'cycles, and also an infinitely variable-ratio gear, made possible by a belt drive onto two conically opposed pulleys, which far outstripped anything else then on the market, and enabled the company's machines to win every race they entered.

In 1934 the mill became the tent and sail works of Mr C. Nielson, and has since been divided among a number of firms, including Robert Vince Advertising, who have done much to get the premises back into good order.

In the census returns of 1841 only one person in Molesey was listed as employed in manufacturing, and that was a man in West Molesey described as a basket maker. For centuries the small islands along the Thames (Budworth's 'willow'd aytes') had been utilised for the cultivation of osiers for baskets and cane furniture. Because the raw material of the trade, the osier rods, were seasonal in supply, much of the labour used was itinerant, and tramped into the district from afar for the annual work. The West Molesey parish register of June 1840 records the baptism of the child of a basket maker all the way from Watford in Hertfordshire.

The Thames provided the district with a variety of employments — ferrymen, fishermen (freshwater fish were at one time highly regarded as a table delicacy), bargemen, boat builders, boat hirers, watermen of every description: jobs which have all but disappeared. It is difficult now to picture the great impact that the river once had on the district, reaching its hey-day in the Edwardian era, and collapsing abruptly with the advent of the motor car. The employees of the Thames Water Authority are nowadays almost the only people to obtain their livelihood from our great northern neighbour.

Gravel and water are about the only exploitable minerals found naturally in Molesey. Gravel was at one time used mainly for metalling the roads, and obtained by dredging the rivers, although two plots of ground were allotted under the Enclosure Award, from which each parish was allowed to dig gravel. When its value as building material became fully appreciated, its extraction became big business. Increasing demand for housing and other development brought increasing pressure on every available site offering access to the precious deposits. Landowners became aware of the fortune which lay under their feet. Within something like forty years, most potential sites were exploited and exhausted, the land reinstated, and covered by houses, schools, factories and playing fields.

A number of other individual industrial undertakings flourished for a time and then faded away. During the 18th century an extensive tanyard was to be found in the grounds of what is now called Old Manor House in Bell Road. The nearby crossing of the river Mole is known as Tanner's Bridge. The tanning pits were said to be still visible less than a hundred years ago. One book on Molesey history records that, further along Bell Road, near to East Molesey Court, 'in the middle of the last century stood a spinning mill, erected to spin wool for the bandages required by the army in the Crimean War'. No verification of this has been possible.

A large house called The Priory, which stood on the site now covered by the houses in Anne Way and Helen Close, was acquired by Messrs J. C. & C. Field Ltd, the well-known makers of candles, for the bleaching of wax for high-class candles, especially those for church use. It first appears in the rate books in 1845. In the 1890s the factory was closed and the wax for Field's candles was imported from the south of France, where the sunlight necessary for the process was infinitely greater than at West Molesey.

A works which existed until recently between Spring Gardens and Avern Road, now developed for housing, had a chequered career. Originally built about the turn of the century by a local firm of builders called Potterton and Gould as a steam-powered saw mill, it was soon taken over by J. J. Griffen and Sons, manufacturers of photographic papers, who stayed here until about 1922. After that it was used by H. S. Whiteside and Company, the makers of Sun Pat Raisins and other sweets, and later by Messrs British Fondants, who considerably enlarged the premises for the milling of almond confectionery.

Since the end of the last war, considerable industrial development has taken place in West Molesey, especially in the Central Avenue/Island Farm Road area, on land which until then had produced nothing but milk and beef cattle. This estate, known locally as Little Pittsburgh, provides employment not only for hundreds of Molesey men and women, but for many from a much wider field as well.

ABOVE: East Molesey Mill, from Hampton Court station, during the flood of 1894. BELOW: Thomas Andrews (1804-1892), owner of the Mill, outside Creek House.

ABOVE: Site of Ember Mill, part in East Molesey and part in Thames Ditton. BELOW: Old Manor House, once the tannery, built by Thomas Willett, probably in 1767.

ABOVE: Outbuildings of The Priory, at one time Field's candle works, and later a nursery. BELOW: Rural Molesey — cows grazing where the West Molesey factory estate now stands.

ABOVE: Bridge Road, about 1900. BELOW: A Christmas display — Mr Biggs' butcher's shop.

ABOVE: Walton Road, about 1910. LEFT: The corn chandler's — Mr Edwin Buteux outside his shop on the corner of Walton Road and Spring Gardens, about the turn of the century. CENTRE: Shops in Bridge Road, about 1930: Thomas Usher, ironmonger; E. Payne, tobacconist, and A. Angus, coal merchant. BELOW: Shops in Walton Road, about 1947, before completion of the Parade.

ABOVE: Walnut Tree House, later East Molesey Lodge, now the site of Cedar Road. BELOW: East Molesey Lodge, Bridge Road, demolished in 1930.

Many Mansions

'A House with lawns enclosing it,
A living river by the door'.
Robert Louis Stevenson
Underwoods (1887)

In the year 1519 Sir Thomas Heneage, Cardinal Wolsey's gentleman usher, wishing to be within call of his eminence, acquired an estate in East Molesey and erected for himself a sumptuous mansion. Thus started a trend which was to continue for several centuries. The position of Molesey, within an easy ride of the metropolis, on the banks of the Thames, on the doorstep of Hampton Court, but in rural sequestration, provided a haven for those whose business required them to be close to the capital, but whose desires were to be free of its dismal smoke-wracked hurly-burly. Even before the accepted commutor age, various people who possessed the means purchased a piece of Molesey and located their country seat here. At the end of the last century the village of West Molesey was surrounded by no less than ten houses large enough to be called mansions. Not one now remains!

The mansion that Sir Thomas Heneage built was probably where Cedar Road is now. A large house remained on the site until 1930, and was said to have vaults of substantial masonry and wide arches of far greater extent than would have been required for the house as it then existed. In the early 19th century it was called Walnut Tree House. In 1853 it was bought by Frederick Lowton Spinks, this country's last serjeant-at-law, given a new classical facade, and renamed East Molesey Lodge. In the grounds stood a large cedar of Lebanon, after which the present roads are named.

When, c1780, the owners of the gunpowder mills became lords of the manors, the mill buildings were demolished, and the mill house, which probably dated from the 17th century (when it was the largest house in East Molesey), was renovated and turned into a country residence. All the land between the river Mole and Walton Road, from Bell Road westward to where Seymour Road now runs, was purchased and transformed into a vast park. Horace Walpole visited the estate in 1795 and wrote of it in one of his letters: 'The situation seems handsome, the house extremely pretty, there is a lovely little gallery painted in trelliage'. From 1821 to 1835 it was owned by Joseph Todd, a haberdasher from London. In true fairytale fashion he started life as an apprentice in a shop, married the owner's daughter, inherited the shop and, when he retired to live the life of a country gentleman at East Molesey, it was with a princely fortune of nearly one million sterling. Todd's descendants sold the estate around 1850 to the Dowager Lady Clinton, on whose death in 1876 the house was demolished and the park developed as a high-class residential estate. The site of the house is now occupied by East Molesey Court, a red brick house, built about 1880 in Jacobean style. In 1927 Molesey Council proposed to adapt it for offices and use the grounds for recreation. It would have cost £12,000, but was turned down. Two years later the house, together with the land on the other side of the Mole, was laid out as a sports ground, firstly for the Distillers Company, and then for the Trollope and Colls Group. On the night of 30 July 1983 a disastrous fire gutted the house; the burnt out hulk still remains a gaunt sight. Its future is unsure.

When East Molesey Park was split up for housing, one lot of some ten acres bordering on the Mole was sold, on condition that only one house was erected thereon and that to be of not less that £4,000 value. The house was designed by the architect Edward Salter for his brother Talford. Unfortunately, due to an error in measuring-out, the builder constructed the house much closer to Molesey Park Road than the original plans showed, and the Local Board seriously considered ordering him to demolish the building and re-erect it in the proper place. However, they let it stay and, when the house was enlarged in 1891, allowed the road to be diverted in a wide loop to permit a garden in front of it. As early as 1781 a part of this plot was known as The Wilderness, and this was adopted as the name of the house. The estate is now the sports ground of the Standard Chartered Bank.

The large 19th century house, now three separate apartments, known as 15, 17 and 19 Arnison Road, once stood in extensive grounds stretching back to Bridge Road, and faced what was then a delightful little footpath through the woods. At one time it was called Strawberry Villa, as no less than an eighth of an acre of the grounds was devoted to the cultivation of this fruit, described in 1870 as 'some of the finest strawberries that were ever put on table', and so prolific, that 382 fruits were picked from just six plants selected at random. The owner was then Mr Alfred Goodman, a successful lawyer, who was also the drum-major for the London Scottish. His kilted figure and dashing aplomb in this role, during the procession to mark the Queen's jubilee, so caught the public eye that it inspired one composer to write what became a one-time popular song *Here comes the great Drum-major*. The name was later changed to Araucaria, which derives from the botanical name for the Chile Pine or Monkey Puzzle tree which dominated the garden.

Of West Molesey's mansions the largest was undoubtedly Hurst House, a pleasant Georgian building, surrounded by grounds and pleasure gardens which covered all the land now occupied by that part of the Hurst Park development south of Hurst Road. The house was probably built at the end of the 18th century for Sir Robert Smyth, baronet, lord of the manor of West Molesey, a one-time Member of Parliament and staunch supporter of Thomas Paine. At the time of the French Revolution he renounced his title and went to live in Paris. During the 19th century it was occupied by a number of different people, most of whose names could be found among the pages of Burke and Debrett. In 1890 the house was purchased by the Hurst Park Racing Club and was for a time used as a clubhouse. It was demolished about 1900. Rows of stables were built on part of the grounds to house the racehorses and, during the last war, with the stalls removed, these were used by the Home Guard as a rifle range.

Next to Hurst House in New Road was what was once quite a large house. Probably also built in the 18th century, it too was owned by the Smyth family, maybe as a dower house to the larger mansion. Later it was occupied by Joseph Palmer, soldier, author, and donor of several West Molesey charities. Born Joseph Budworth, he served for a time in the army, rising to the rank of Captain. From action at the siege of Gibraltar he carried wounds to his dying day. He married a rich Irish lady, Elizabeth Palmer, and retired to live at West Molesey. When, through his wife, he inherited large estates in Ireland, he changed his name to Palmer. But in spite of his new found affluence he still preferred to live quietly in this small house in Molesey rather than in either of the massive mansions in the Emerald Isle which he possessed. One of his poems, *On Simplicity*, part of which is quoted as the prologue to this book, tells of rural life in 'Dear Peaceful Molesey'. He was a great campaigner for control of child labour, and one of his books, *The Lancashire Collier Girl*, tells of a little girl forced to go down the mines and dig coal in order to bring up her orphaned brothers and sisters. Palmer presented the village of West Molesey with the clock which still chimes the hours from the church tower, and gave money to provide Christmas cheer for the poor, which is still paid. He died in 1815 and lies buried in the churchyard. At that time the house was called Mole Cottage. It was purchased by Sir Robert Carden, Lord Mayor of London and Member of Parliament, considerably enlarged in battlemented Gothic style, and renamed Mole Lodge. Its later name, Mole Abbey, dates from the beginning of this century, and was probably inspired by the appearance of Carden's additions. As with all West Molesey's mansions it was pulled down for development.

Further along Hurst Road, standing in five acres of ground, now occupied by Wilton Gardens, was Hurstside. Its most distinguished resident was Sir Henry Thompson (1820-1909), a noted surgeon, who was one of the first to operate successfully for the removal of gall-stones. He operated on both the King of the Belgians and Napoleon III. His talents in other fields were many: he was an amateur astronomer of no mean ability and had an observatory at Hurstside which included a telescope twice the size of any then in use. He was an excellent artist, a writer of novels, a collector of china, and his interest in hygiene led him to become one of the first in this country to advocate and popularise cremation, culminating in the formation of the crematorium at Golders Green. He bitterly opposed the extension of the cemetery at West Molesey, which ironically brought graves almost to his back door.

Where Grange Road now runs there stood another Georgian mansion, The Grange, probably built for Sir Richard Sutton MP, Under-Secretary of State in Pitt's administration, who bought up several pieces of land around 1772. The estate of some 15 acres extended from Walton Road to Beauchamp Road. The house was originally called Elm Lodge, but in 1843 was bought by a barrister named Edmund Lionel Wells who gave it its later name. In 1903 the whole estate was taken over by the building firm of A. & F. Jury of Tooting, who commenced erecting houses. The development was halted by the First World War. In 1928 Molesey Council took some of the land for the erection of municipal housing (most of which has recently been demolished and rebuilt). The old house itself was turned into flats, and a large ornamental lake of over an acre in extent gradually filled in. At the end of the Second World War, the rest of the estate was bought by the Council, the mansion was pulled down, and the process of development continued. The site of the house is now occupied by Brende Gardens.

Immediately adjacent to The Grange, on the ground now occupied by Molesey Football Club and the surrounding roads, was The Priory. In May 1785 this estate was the venue for one of the earliest balloon flights in England. James Sadler, the first English-born aeronaut, went up with William Wyndham MP, in a flight which they hoped would take them to France, but which the wind decreed would drop them in the mouth of the river Thames instead. It was acquired around 1845 by Messrs Field and the outbuildings used for the treatment of wax for candles. The house was demolished during the 1930s.

In High Street, where the present house-mother scheme for the elderly called Manor Court stands, was the oldest and most interesting of West Molesey's great houses. Probably dating from the late 16th century, although much altered and enlarged later, it was a rambling house, partly brick and partly weatherboard, of great character, full of attics, gables, and little extensions, and with a fine staircase curving around a central wooden pillar running right up to the top of the house like a great ship's mast. The house may have been West Molesey's original manor house; indeed during the latter part of its life it was called Old Manor House, although for decades prior to the 1930s its name was The Limes, and before that Ivy Cottage.

Two mansions about which little requires to be said were to be found on either side of Walton Road at the far western end of the parish — Ivy Lodge on the south side where Tonbridge Road is now; and Sutton Lodge (otherwise Sutton Villa) on the north side. Ivy Lodge was built about 1850 and demolished in the 1930s. The life of Sutton Lodge almost spanned the 19th century; its site is now covered by the waters of the Bessborough Reservoir.

An older and much more interesting house was The Lodge, formerly Moulsey Villa, which stood just to the south of Ivy Lodge, off what is now Molesey Road. A house stood on this site at least from the 18th century and probably well before that. Here lived an eminent distiller named Jenkin Jones, who insured part of the premises in 1781, but was killed four years later by a fall from his horse. Another early resident was Sir Stephen Shairp, who retired here after being British ambassador to Russia. His daughter married Captain Marryatt of *Midshipman Easy* fame. At one time the house served as a seminary, catering for 17 young ladies. It then became the home of Dr John Cockle, a noted Victorian physician, whose daughter presented the lych-gate to West Molesey Church in his memory. It was later re-named Monks' Pool. The coach-house and outbuildings stood as Rose Cottages until 1973, when they made way for the construction of The Dene housing estate.

The last mansion to fall to the demolition contractor's hammer was The Grove, in Walton Road. In the 18th and early 19th centuries it was owned by the Palmer family, lords of the manor of Walton, and occupied for a while by Colonel Hotham, son of one Lord Hotham and father of another. In 1829 the house was remodelled by the architect Decimus Burton for the Rt Hon John Wilson Croker, Secretary to the Admiralty, Member of Parliament, and Privy Counsellor. Croker was a noted politician and man of letters in the first half of the 19th century, and the man who is generally credited with suggesting the name Conservative for the old Tory Party. The house later devolved on the Barrow family. Around 1932 the estate was turned into a sports club for Faraday House Electrical College. During the last war it was used as a British Restaurant and afterwards reverted to a sports ground for Bentalls, the Kingston store. After this the place was sold to Elmbridge Council for housing purposes and, after considerable discussion had taken place on whether it should be preserved or not, the problem was opportunely solved in May 1975 when yet another mysterious nocturnal conflagration engulfed the building. Before night fell again, bulldozers razed the last of Molesey's great houses to the ground.

The garden of East Molesey Lodge, showing the cedar of Lebanon after which Cedar Road is named.

AT A LOW RESERVE.

By Order of Trustees and others.

EAST MOLESEY.

About five minutes' walk from Hampton Court Station, within a short distance of the District Council Offices and Fire Station.

Particulars and Conditions of Sale of

AN OLD-FASHIONED

FREEHOLD HOUSE,

KNOWN AS

"Holly Lodge," Walton Rd.,

Containing 12 Rooms, and having a Large Garden at rear extending to the Watercourse.

ALSO THE

Monumental Mason's Yard

ADJOINING, TOGETHER WITH THE

WORKSHOPS THEREON.

Which will be Sold by Auction, by Messrs.

Nightingale, Phillips & Page

At "THE CASTLE" HOTEL, EAST MOLESEY,

On TUESDAY, JULY 16th, 1901,

AT 7 O'CLOCK IN THE EVENING,
IN ONE LOT, IF NOT SOLD, IN TWO LOTS.

SOLICITORS:—
Messrs. CANN & SON,
33, Gracechurch Street, E.C., and East Molesey.
AND
R. JENNINGS, Esq.,
28, Basinghall Street, E.C.

AUCTIONEERS:—
Messrs. NIGHTINGALE, PHILLIPS & PAGE,
Eagle Chambers, Kingston-upon-Thames,
Telephone—Kingston 27; Weybridge 4.   And at WEYBRIDGE.

ABOVE: Captain Lionel de Sausmarez RN; resident of East Molesey Lodge. RIGHT: Catalogue of sale of Holly Lodge, Walton Road, 1901. BELOW: Admiral the Hon Sir George Cranfield Berkeley (1753-1818), former resident of Hurst House, buried in West Molesey Church.

ABOVE: Radnor House, Walton Road, one of East Molesey's delightful Georgian houses, demolished by Esher Council in 1963. BELOW: The Wilderness, now the sports ground of the Standard Chartered Bank; built in 1881 and enlarged in 1891.

ABOVE: Mole Abbey, New Road, now the site of Mole Abbey Gardens.
BELOW: New Road, showing the position of the former Mole Abbey; on the left, the stables of Hurst Park racecourse.

WEST MOLESEY, SURREY.

About 1½ miles from Hampton Court Station; within easy reach of Hurst Park, Kempton Park, Sandown Park, Esher, Teddington, and a short distance from the River.

THE PARTICULARS AND CONDITIONS OF SALE

OF THE IMPORTANT

Freehold Residential Estate

KNOWN AS

"MOLE LODGE,"

In excellent order, standing in beautifully laid out and **well-timbered GROUNDS**, in all about

12½ ACRES,

With First Class Stabling, Three Coach Houses and Coachman's Quarters, Gardener's Lodge, Handsome Conservatory, Ranges of Glass Houses, Various other Outbuildings, Paddocks, &c.

MESSRS.

J. A. LUMLEY & CO.

Have been favoured with instructions from the Owner, to offer the above BY AUCTION,

At the MART, TOKENHOUSE YARD, LONDON, E.C.,

ON WEDNESDAY, THE 27th DAY OF JULY, 1898,

At ONE o'clock precisely *(unless previously disposed of by Private Treaty).*

Particulars and Conditions of Sale may be obtained of Messrs. MURRAY, HUTCHINS, STIRLING AND MURRAY, Solicitors, 11, Birchin Lane, London, E.C.; at the MART, Tokenhouse Yard, E.C.; and of the Auctioneers,

J. A. LUMLEY & Co., "Lumley House," 34, St. James's Street, London, S.W.

Sale catalogue for Mole Lodge, later Mole Abbey.

LEFT: Sir Robert Carden (1801-1888), one time Lord Mayor of London, and resident of Mole Lodge. BELOW: Mole Abbey Cottage, once known as Grove Cottage, before conversion by the Rosemary Simmonds Memorial Housing Association into homes for elderly people. RIGHT: Sir Henry Thompson (1820-1904), one time resident of Hurstside'.

ABOVE: The Grange, demolished about 1948; the site is now occupied by Brende Gardens. BELOW: The Grange, from the south, showing the ornamental lake, about one acre in extent.

ABOVE: Old Manor House, formerly The Limes, High Street; demolished by Esher Council in 1963, and BELOW: the staircase.

ABOVE: Old Manor House, the rear gables. LEFT: Edward Jesse (1780-1860), naturalist and writer, lived at one time in the house which later became West Molesey Vicarage. RIGHT: 'The Beautiful Miss Croker', sister-in-law and adopted daughter of John Wilson Croker, later Lady Barrow, died in 1906 aged 96 years.

ABOVE: The Grove, designed by Decimus Burton in 1829, demolished by Elmbridge Council in 1975; front and BELOW: rear view.

LEFT: Bookplate of Rt Hon John Wilson Croker, owner of The Grove, 1829-1857.
RIGHT: Lieut Gen Sir Robert Walpole (1808-1876), died at The Grove, and buried in West Molesey churchyard.
BELOW: Ivy Lodge, demolished about 1936, the site now occupied by Tonbridge Road.

ABOVE: The Lodge, now the site of The Dene housing estate, and
BELOW: stables and outbuildings, demolished in 1975.

WEST MOLESEY, SURREY.

Within a pleasant walk of Hampton Court Station and the River Thames.

Particulars, Plan and Conditions of Sale

OF A VERY DESIRABLE

FREEHOLD ESTATE

COMPRISING A TOTAL AREA OF ABOUT

15a. 0r. 7p.

AND INCLUDING A COMMODIOUS

OLD-FASHIONED RESIDENCE

KNOWN AS

"THE LODGE,"

Encircled by beautifully timbered and secluded

Pleasure Grounds, Gardens & Paddocks

WITH

SUMMER HOUSE, LODGE, GARDENER'S COTTAGE,

GREENHOUSES, STABLING and OUTBUILDINGS,

AND A

LONG FRONTAGE UPON THE ROAD TO ESHER AND WALTON

Within a short distance of West Molesey Church and Post and Telegraph Office.

The whole Free of Tithe Rentcharge and Land Tax.

POSSESSION ON COMPLETION.

Which will be Sold by Auction,

BY

WEATHERALL & GREEN

At the Auction Mart, Tokenhouse Yard, E.C.,

On TUESDAY, the 25th day of JUNE, 1901,

At ONE o'Clock.—IN ONE LOT.

Messrs. PERKINS & WESTON,
Solicitors,
9, *Gray's Inn Square,* W.C.

LEFT: Sale catalogue of The Lodge, 1901. ABOVE: High House, No 154 Bridge Road, about 1910; this house has recently been restored and the front door returned to the position on the left. RIGHT: Lorne Cottage, High Street, demolished about 1960.

ABOVE: West Molesey village, around 1900. BELOW: Early 19th century cottages in Bell Road.

ABOVE: Wolsey Road in Edwardian times; no cars, only dogs. BELOW: Walton Road, about 1930.

ABOVE: Hurst Road in flood, 1906. BELOW: New Road before road widening.

The Castle Hotel and old Hampton Court bridge from the river Mole. Note in the top left hand corner the bridge which connected the main building to the annex constructed in 1887. BELOW: Castle Hotel, from the river.

There is a Tavern

'There is nothing which has yet been contrived
by man by which so much happiness is produced
as by a good tavern or inn'.
              Samuel Johnson (21 March 1776)

In 1636 John Taylor, better known as a waterman-poet, compiled a *vade-mecum* for travellers entitled *A Catalogue of Tavernes in Ten Shires about London,* and gave us our earliest known record of public houses in Molesey. He notes first 'At Mowlessey, Anthony Powell'. This presumably refers to East Molesey, as an Anthony Powell was for some time a warden of East Molesey Church. But where he resided and what his house was called we do not know. Taylor then continues 'At Little Moulesey, Parnell Nitingale, White Hart'. The White Hart was almost certainly the forerunner of the Royal Oak at West Molesey. The Nightingale family was established in the parish for many generations, mostly as yeoman farmers, and filled many parochial offices.

By the middle seventeen hundreds there were three public houses flourishing in East Molesey — The Castle, by the riverside adjacent to Hampton Court ferry; The Bell, opposite the parish church; and The Swan, near Tanners Bridge. Because of Molesey's river-girt situation, the villages saw virtually no through traffic, and the Castle was probably the only house catering for travellers and thereby qualifying as an inn. The other two would have been alehouses providing only for the needs of locals.

The Swan occupied a position at the farther end of a row of cottages, which then stretched from the house now called Quillets Royal to the roadway leading to Tanners Bridge. From an insurance policy taken out in 1758 we find it was a timber building, probably of weather-board construction, of two storeys, 37 by 19 feet. As early as 1737, however, the churchwardens bought beer from the landlord, William Hollis, probably to refresh the bell-ringers.

The earliest mention of the Bell is in 1706, when a coroner's inquest on the body of a man killed in an explosion at the gunpowder mill was held there. Although the house was larger than the Swan, it seems primarily to have been a farmhouse, known for much of the 18th century as St Eloy's Farm, and the farmer only ran the alehouse as a secondary consideration. In fact it continued as such until 1777, when John Goddard, who had previously been mine host at the Swan, moved to take over the Bell. Goddard was apparently no farmer and concentrated purely on running the public house. The Swan then closed its doors as a pub.

The many-gabled facade of the Bell, its medley of warped shapes, its twisted angles and rippling roof, its patterned bargeboards and seemingly unopenable windows, have created a paradise for artists and photographers alike. The Dickensian atmosphere absolutely reeks of mail coaches and masked highwaymen, and such allure is bound to generate romantic legends. The dandified Claude Duval, whose particular haunt was Hounslow Heath just across the river, and Jerry Abershaw, who terrified the Portsmouth Road until he was hanged in 1795, are the two gentlemen of the road whose names are most usually associated with the Bell by storytellers; even the legendary Turpin is not entirely left out of their accounts. Truth to tell, however, all of these tales, romantic though they may be, must remain pure speculation. There is no authentic evidence to link any of them with the Bell at all, and most likely none of them ever even saw the place.

The Castle stood abutting the eastern side of Bridge Road, directly fronting the banks of both the Thames and the Mole, on the space now occupied by the roundabout in front of the Ferryboat Inn. (At that time Hampton Court bridge formed a continuation of Bridge Road and the Mole disgorged into the Thames where Hampton Court Way now runs.) When the house was first built is not certain; it was here in the reign of George I, for it is shown in the background of Leonard Knyff's bird's eye view of the Palace, and on many other prints and paintings. Its *raison d'être* was probably to cater for travellers wanting to cross the ferry, who would demand refreshment or a night's lodging.

In 1816 the Castle, together with a lot of other property in Molesey, was put up for sale. Its relative value can be appreciated by the fact that this lot sold for £1,000, while the Bell, including an adjacent shop, two cottages and gardens, fetched a mere £550. Moreover, the Bell, which is often thought of as an old coaching inn, had only half the stable accommodation of the Castle, and no coach-house.

When the original Hampton Court bridge was constructed in 1753, certain roads were laid down as an approach for travellers coming from the Portsmouth Road, including that now known as Esher Road. The inevitable increase of traffic engendered by this new road appears to have been the stimulus for the opening of another hostelry. This was sited in what had previously been a shop at the junction of the new road and Walton Road, opposite the present police station, on what is at the moment derelict land, and was called The Bridge Coffee House.

We should not be misled by the use of the term Coffee House. As Defoe informs us: 'when you come into them they are but ale houses only they think that the name of coffee house gives them a better air'. It was presumably this better air that the proprietor, a Joseph Carpenter, was aiming at, for he describes himself not as an innkeeper but as a vintner — a seller of wines, probably thinking that the clientele to which he aspired was more used to sipping wine in the comfort of a coffee house than quaffing ale in a common taproom.

That he did, in fact, draw upon the custom of the upper crust is demonstrated by the diary of John Baker, formerly Solicitor-General of the Leeward Islands, who records that, on 7 August 1769: 'I went to Garrick's house, thence by boat near the bridge and dined Bridge Coffee House, Moulsey'. There the two were joined by a party which included Sir Thomas Frederick, of Burwood Park, Hersham; Henry Dodwell, of the Priory, West Molesey; James Norman, the owner of the gunpowder mills; Mr Rowlls, the Kingston brewer, and Edward Lovibond, the poet. That such company should choose this establishment for their carousal shows that, within a remarkably short space of time, it had already secured a high reputation for good fare.

Joseph Carpenter was not the only person to realise the potential of this area for opening a hostelry. Just across the road there was a large cottage with a garden running down to the river Mole, and this was leased to a man named John Benham who, about 1766, obtained a licence to open it as a public house, and called it the Kings Arms. It soon became part of the community life of the village. The Parish Vestry minute book recalls that, on 22 September

1767, the meeting was adjourned to the 'House of John Benham', which it further describes as 'one of the usual Houses of meeting'. The Bridge Coffee House closed down not long after that.

In the 18th and early 19th centuries public houses were the very focal point of village social activity. The publicans, too, played an important and respected role in local affairs. Their names are often to be found in the lists of Molesey's parochial officers, as churchwardens, overseers and the like. In 1845 the horse omnibus to London called every morning (except Sundays) at the Royal Oak and the Kings Arms to pick up passengers, and every evening to set them down again. Twice a week the carrier, William James from Weybridge, with his lumbering van, called at the same two hostelries to collect parcels and such human cargo as could not afford the luxury of the omnibus. It is not without significance that in both East and West Molesey it was an inn which became the village's first post office. Mine hosts were both innkeepers and postmasters alike, often delivering the mail to the houses themselves. As there were then no letter boxes, people had to take their letters to the pub and post them in mail bags, which were hung up in the bar-rooms; this they could do up to a quarter past six in the evening, but late postings could be accepted up to half past six on payment of an extra one penny each.

In 1830 an Act was passed which enabled the owner of any property assessed above a certain value to obtain a licence to sell beer (and only beer). The first of such beerhouses in Molesey was opened at the end of a terrace of cottages in Bridge Road known as Bridge Row. In 1839 this was acquired by William Shaw, the owner of a brewery business in Church Street, Kingston, called Albion Brewery, and from this the beerhouse, which was managed by a middle-aged woman name Sarah Evans, was called The Albion.

Propitiously, the opening of the Albion coincided with two other events which were to have a profound effect on the development of the district and its pubs — the opening of Hampton Court Palace to the public and the building of the branch railway. These together were the catalyst to draw thousands of people to the area, providing a ready reservoir of potential customers for any public house in the immediate neighbourhood — a situation of which entrepreneurs were not slow to take advantage. Thus, at the end of the century, no less than five public houses and one licensed restaurant were located within 100 yards of the foot of the bridge, where only one, the Castle, had existed before.

The first new public house to appear after the opening of the railway was built on a plot of land almost opposite the Albion, and opened in 1853. Of a rather flamboyant Victorian Tudor style, it was at first called the Prince of Wales and Railway Hotel and, although the latter part of the name was soon dropped, it appears on the first 25 inch Ordnance Map as just The Railway Hotel.

Barely 14 years elapsed before the next inn appeared in Bridge Road, and was given the name Carnarvon Castle, although no reason for the choice is obvious; the Anglicised spelling is surely unlikely to have been adopted by a Welshman. It stood next to the Castle and on the way to and from the railway station. This was ideal for passing traffic and, as it was announced that the railway alone had bought three quarters of a million people to Hampton Court during the previous year, the potential trade was enormous. As originally constructed, the building was surmounted by a small decorative turret, which was removed about 40 years ago.

During the 1880s the popularity of the riverside grew apace, bringing more and more visitors and more and more business to the catering trade. Little wonder that Mr Charles Dickens, the son of the novelist, wrote of Molesey that it was chiefly interesting to excursionists from the point of view of refreshment. The Carnarvon Castle was enlarged in 1883 and again in 1895. Not to be outdone, the owners of the Castle built an annex on a piece of ground between their house and the Carnarvon, which consisted of dining rooms, a billiard room, and bedrooms. It was a plain, rather hideous building. Its biggest drawback was a public road which isolated it from the main building. This problem was overcome by the construction of a bridge over the road, virtually a covered corridor, forming a passage linking the two premises at second floor level.

In 1887, the same year that the Castle's annex was built, further development was proceeding on the opposite side of the road. Mr Harry Tagg, a member of the well-known family of watermen, had a boat works along River Bank, in a building which had been erected in the 1870s, and which still stands on the corner of Feltham Avenue (although that road had not then been constructed). He also had a house in Bridge Road which backed onto the works, part of which he used as refreshment rooms. In the crutch between was an open field, known locally as Griffen's Corner. Mr Tagg was nothing if not a businessman and, realising the value of the site, treated for a lease of the field. He then demolished the house, moving the refreshment rooms to the top storey of his boat works with a verandah overlooking the river, and built a magnificent hotel on the whole corner, which he named the Thames Hotel. To all and sundry it was known simply as Tagg's Hotel, and was so called by locals, as the present writer recalls, long after its founder was dead and buried.

Meanwhile, down in the village of East Molesey, the resident population was steadily growing, providing ever-increasing possibilities for the expansion of licensed business. In the middle decades of the century three new public houses were opened along Walton Road. Initially each opened as a beerhouse under the 1830 Act, and each straightaway applied for a full licence to serve wines and spirits, but each had to wait, in some cases several years, before this was actually granted. A licence was allowed for the New Inn in 1856, for the Europa in 1861, and for the Poyntz Arms in 1868.

The Royal Oak is one of the most popular of all English pub names, and commemorates the escape of King Charles after the Battle of Worcester, concealed in the famous Boscobel Oak. Our West Molesey Royal Oak must have been among the earliest of these, for we know it to have been so called as early as 1669, when the landlord, Robert Curtis, had his own halfpenny tokens minted because of the dearth of small coinage. Before this, as we have already stated, it was known as the White Hart. The old inn was a rambling weather-boarded timber building, which stood until the middle of the last century. It was demolished and the present house erected probably soon after it was taken over by Hodgson's Kingston Brewery in 1857.

The present house called The Cannon in High Street dates from 1897, but replaces a much older building. The earliest mention of this is in 1753.

On the corner of High Street and Walton Road, where the post office and grocer's shop now stands, there were formerly five cottages, built about 1810, the largest of which became a beerhouse called The Traveller's Friend. In 1867 the Beerhouse Act was repealed and the landlords of all those houses which had opened under the old act now had to obtain annual licences from the magistrates at the Brewster Sessions. As far as the Traveller's Friend was concerned, the bench did this reluctantly and only after their worships had given the landlord a strict warning to be very particular not to engage in Sunday trading. At this time the licensee, William Heirsey, combined the business of beer retailing with that of butcher, selling beer on one side of the passage and meat on the other. Three years later, all the property on this corner was demolished for road widening, as part of an agreement with the Lambeth Water Company, who were laying their mains. And that was the end of the Traveller's Friend.

Around 1870 John Cann, the Clerk to the East Molesey Local Board, developed an area of land just inside West Molesey parish, on which he laid down a road and built houses. Realising the commercial possibilities of a public house midway between the two Moleseys, in an area ripe for development, Mr Cann had a house built on the corner of the road suitable for use as an inn, and in March 1870 applied for a full licence, which the bench declined to entertain.

He then applied for a beerhouse certificate, but met with no better success. He then applied for permission to sell beer for consumption off the premises, and this was granted, but withdrawn in the following year after the landlord, John Lawrence, had been convicted of allowing the beer he had sold to be drunk on the premises. The house was then closed up. Every year Lawrence made a fresh application for a licence, and every year with regular monotony it was turned down. It was not until 1882 that the beerhouse certificate was granted and not until well into this century that a full licence was obtained. The house was named after Lord Hotham, the lord of the manors of Molesey, who died in the year it was first built.

After the appearance of the Lord Hotham no new public houses were opened in Molesey for almost a century, and then two sprang up in just over six years — The Paddock in 1968, and The Surveyor in 1974, both built to cater for the residential and industrial growth of West Molesey around that time.

Of the Molesey inns whose stories we have traced, it has been the lot of two to be pulled down for road improvements; two reverted to private houses but both have since been demolished, and three have changed their names. It is sad to relate that the Carnarvon Castle has become the Ferryboat Inn; Tagg's Thames Hotel, The Streets of London; and quite recently the Poyntz Arms has emerged as the Village Arms. This is all to be regretted, but is a sign, one supposes, of changing times and changing social habits, and changes in the role that public houses play in the life of the community.

Castle Hotel, from Bridge Road.

ABOVE: View from the Middlesex bank, showing the Castle Hotel with the annex behind, the two little wooden bridges which spanned the river Mole leading to the station, and on the right hand side behind the bridge, Tagg's Thames Hotel. LEFT: Olde Home, formerly The Bridge Coffee House, and RIGHT: in demolition, 1967, for road improvements, which have yet to take place.

ABOVE: The Albion, opened in the 1830s. LEFT: A Victorian view of the Prince of Wales, opened in 1853. RIGHT: The New Inn, about 1920.

ABOVE: The Europa, about 1920, when it still had a porticoed entrance; Mr Harry Wood's horse and cart stands in front of his greengrocer's shop. BELOW: The Poyntz Arms, about the turn of the century; no motor cars to be seen, but plenty of horse droppings.

ABOVE: Tagg's Thames Hotel, resplendent with tubs and hanging baskets filled with flowers of every hue, and BELOW: The Hotel and boat house from the river.

ABOVE: Bridge Road, about 1880, showing the old bridge, the Castle Hotel, and the Carnavon Castle (now the Ferryboat Inn) with the little turret with which it was formerly crowned. The shops on the western side of the road had not then been built. BELOW: Bridge Road, from the foot of the bridge, about 1900, showing the Thames Hotel and the Carnavon Castle.

118

ABOVE: Bridge Road, showing the tower which once stood atop the Carnarvon Castle (now the Ferryboat Inn). BELOW: The Cannon, rebuilt in 1897.

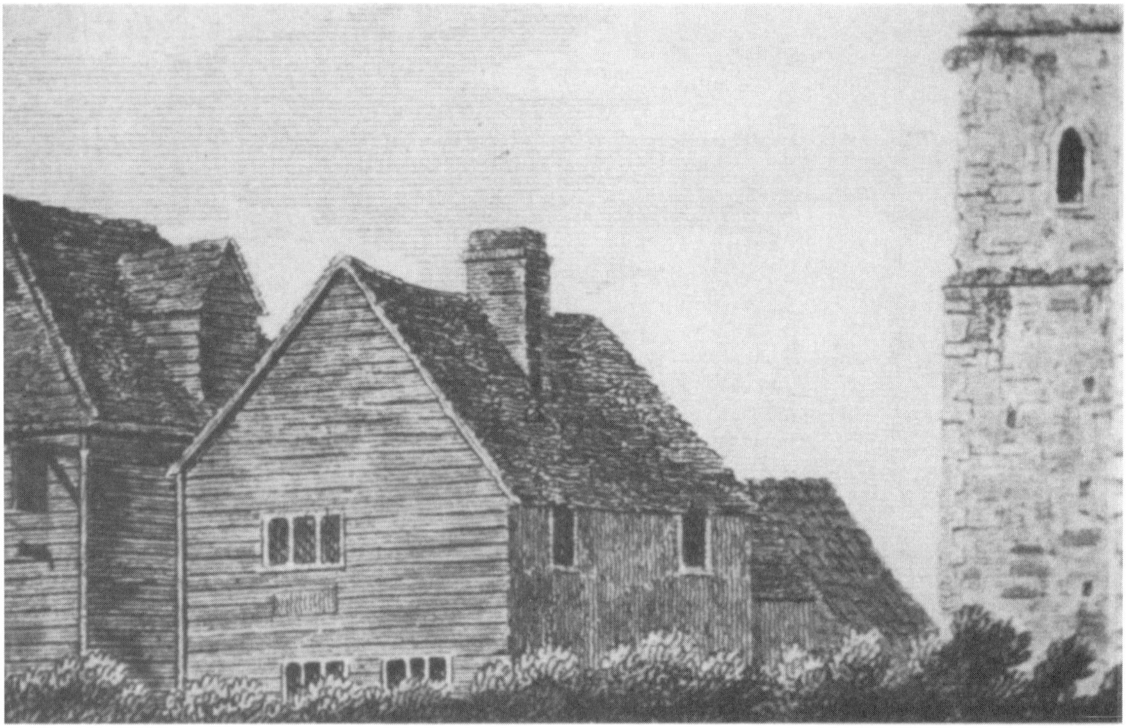

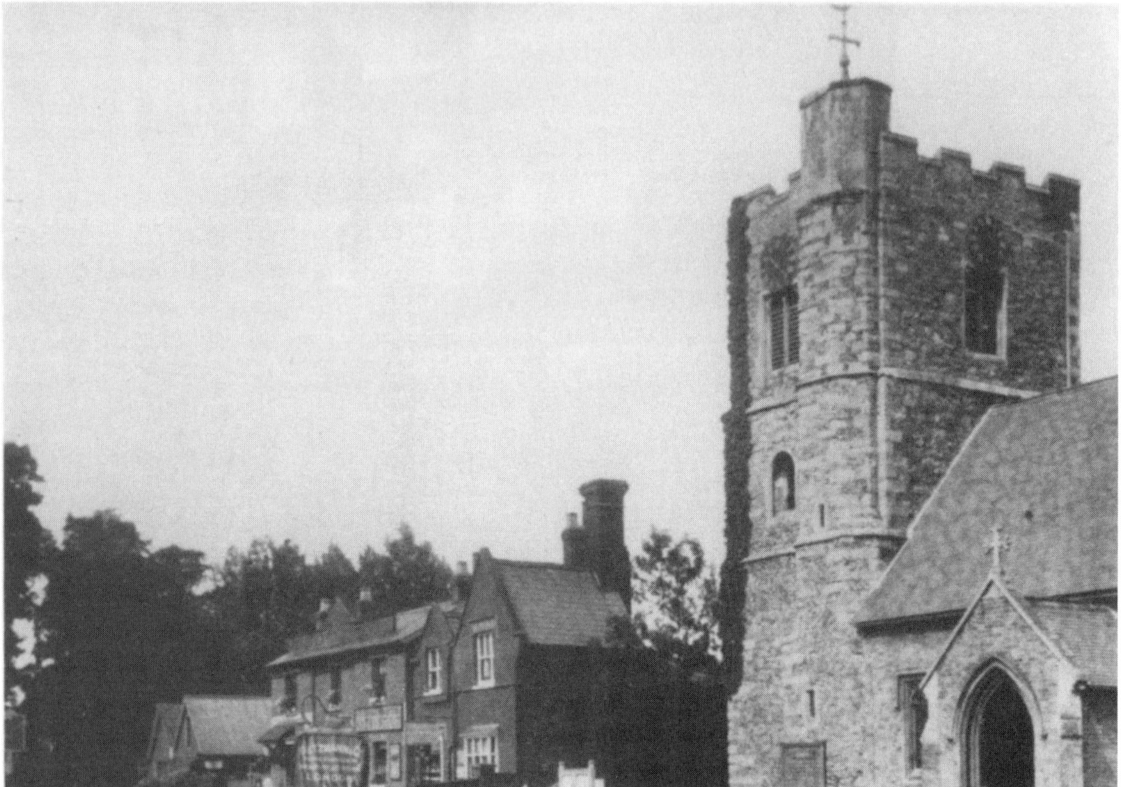

OPPOSITE ABOVE: The old Royal Oak, about 1800, and BELOW: about 1900. ABOVE and RIGHT: The Surveyor looks through his theodolite from the last pub to be built in Molesey.

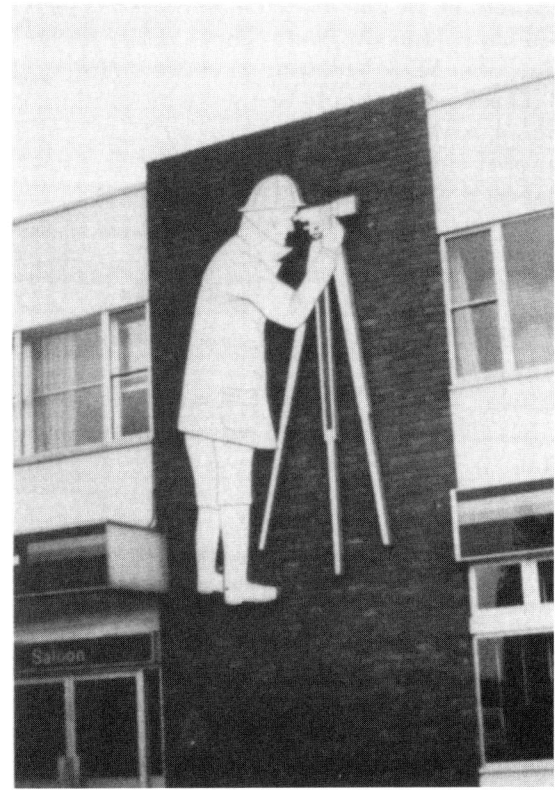

Bibliography

Manuscript Sources

The chief source of manuscripts available to the public is the Surrey Record Office at Kingston, which includes copies of the parish registers and of census returns on microfilm. Other parochial records remain in the care of the respective churches. The proceedings of the succeeding local authorities are now in the custody of Elmbridge Borough Council.

A few documents relating to Molesey are located in the Guildford Muniment Room, the Minet Library at Camberwell, and the Manuscripts Room of the British Library. Some local houses are mentioned in the registers of the old fire insurance offices, now deposited in the Guildhall Library. Surrey wills previous to 1857 can be found in the Greater London Record Office and the Public Record Office.

Printed Works

Molesey

Rambler (Joseph Budworth) *A View of the village of Hampton from Moulsey Hurst* 1797

The Mole (Herbert Andrews) *A Short History of East Molesey* 1893 A rather whimsically written work, but valuable in some respects.

Daniels, H. G. *East and West Molesey, with their surroundings* Homeland Handbooks, 1907

Williams, James *St Paul's Church, East Molesey* 1951

Hawkins, M. & Webster, T. *A Short History of Molesey* Molesey Residents' Association, 1966 This booklet should be used with caution; its 32 pages contain over 90 errors.

Berry, Arthur & Hilda *Charities of Molesey* Molesey Residents' Association, 1969

Brightfield, Myron F. *John Wilson Croker* 1940

Baker, R. G. M. *East and West Molesey, A Dictionary of Local History* 2nd edn 1975

Surrey

Aubrey, John *The Natural History and Antiquities of the County of Surrey* 1718-19, reprinted 1975

Manning, Owen & Bray, William *History and Antiquities of the County of Surrey* 1804-14 The British Library has an extra-illustrated edition of the work, which contains many views of Molesey

Brayley, E. W. & Britton, J. *Topographical History of Surrey* 1841-50 Wimbledon Public Library has an extra-illustrated copy of this work, with some views of Molesey

Malden, H. E. (ed) *A History of the County of Surrey* Victoria History, 1902-14

Cracklow, J. C. T. *Views of Surrey Churches* 1823 reprinted 1975

Gover, J. E. B. and others *The Place Names of Surrey* 1934

Surrey Archaeological Collections: 75 volumes 1858-)

Newspapers

Surrey Comet (1854-)
Surrey Herald (1892-) Esher and Molesey edn from 1963
Molesey Weekly Record (April-June 1935)
Molesey Advertiser (1946-1948)
Molesey and Ditton News (1948-1962)
Molesey News (1968-)

By Order of the Trustees of F. J. KENT, deceased.

EAST MOLESEY and HAMPTON

Particulars and Conditions of Sale of

The Remaining Portions of the Kent Estate

comprising

Freehold Investments in Shops & Houses

let on leases, yearly and weekly tenancies, and producing approximately £1,450 per annum

Freehold Ground Rents of £102 : 6 : 6 per ann.

secured on main road shops, land and houses with early reversions in from 10 to 30 years

---

Well Situated Freehold Building Land Industrial Riverside Land and Premises

The well-known Thames Island known as

ASH ISLAND

adjacent to Molesey Lock

which

A. G. BONSOR
---

is instructed to sell by auction at

The PRINCE OF WALES HOTEL, East Molesey

on Wednesday, 4th December, 1946

at 3.0 p.m.

Particulars and Conditions of Sale may be obtained from Mr. H. W. K. Calder, Solicitor, Messrs. Francis & Calder, Ridgway House, 41-42, King William Street, London, E.C.4, and of the Auctioneer at his offices

82, Eden Street, Kingston.   **72, Victoria Road, Surbiton.**
KINgston 0022-3.   ELMbridge 1522-3.

It was the Kent Estate that started suburbia in Molesey in 1848, and it was in 1946, almost a century later, that the remnants were sold — here is the catalogue of the sale of the last portions of the Kent Estate, 4 December 1946.

Index

Figures in *italics* refer to illustrations

Abernon, Normandy 18
Acts of Parliament
  Beerhouse Act (1830) 111,112
  Claremont Estate Act (1816) 19
  Fire Services Act (1947) 68
  Hampton Court Chase Act (1539) 24
  Hampton Court Gas Act (1867) 67
  Inclosure Act (1815) 80
  Kingston Vicarage Act (1769) 50
  Lambeth Water Act (1871) 67
  Metropolitan Police Act (1900) 68
  Poor Law Amendment Act (1834) 60
  Second Reform Act (1867) 28
  South Western Railway Act (1844) 27
aerial view 74
Alderton, George 4
Andrews, Thomas 83
Angus, Capt A. 71,*87*
Arbelastarius, Simon 18
  W. 18
Arnison, family 27
  John 29
Araucaria 90
Ashby's Bank 31
Aulric 15
Avern Works 82
Balastarius, Odard .. 17,18,*49*
ballooning 91
Baker, John 110
Barnes, Fred 81
Barrow, family 92
  Lady (Miss Croker) . 69,*100*
Barry, Charles 18
basket making 81,*82*
Beckford, Anne 60
Bedwell, Frederick 61
Benham, John 110,111
Benn's Cottage *32*
Benson, Hezekiah 49
Bent, John 61
Bentalls 92
Berkeley, Adm Sir George Cranfield 93
Bigg's butcher's shop *86*
Bonar, B.J. 77
boundaries 79
boundary stone *12*
Brende, Thomas 18,51,*56*
Bridge House 49,68
British Fondants Ltd 82
  Legion *46*,76
  Restaurant 92
Bronze Age *12*,14
Brookwood Necropolis 29
burial ground 29,30
Burton, Decimus 92,*101*
Bury, Thomas Talbot 50
Buteux, Edwin *87*
candle factory 82,*85*
Cann, John 61,112
Carden, Sir Robert 91,*97*

Carpenter, Charles 49
  Joseph 110
Casey Bridge *26*
Charlotte, Princess 19
Chertsey 14,15
  Abbey 15,16,49
Chubb, Mr 51
Churches and Chapels
  Baptist 51
  Methodist 51,69,*75*
  Roman Catholic 52
  St Francis 51
  Mary's ... 14,18,29,49,50, 52,53,69
  Junior Cricket Club *48*
  Paul's . 29,49,50,57,*58*,68
    football team *47*
  Peter's 15,50,51,*55*,*56*
Church Farm 30,*39*
Churchfield 79
Clare, Richard de 17
Claremont 19
Clarke, family 18
  Sir James 19
  Capt John 49
  Joseph 18
Clinton, Lady 30,89
  Lord 30
Coal and Wine Tax post ... *64*
coat of arms *126*
Cobham 14,24,62
cocoa factory 81
Cockle, Dr John 92
Cole, Newdon 60
Colena Ladies Outfitters .. 67
common fields 79,80
Conservative Association .. 61
  Hall 52
Cotton, Sir Richard 18
Cow Common 79
Crabstile Field 79
Creek Cottages 52
  House 73,*83*
Croker, Rt Hon John Wilson 50,55,92,*102*
  'The Beautiful Miss' (Lady Barrow) *100*
Crossfield 79
Croydon 81
Curtis, Robert 112
d'Abernon, Engleram 19
  family 19
  Jordan 19
  Roger 18
Dennes, George Edgar 28
Derrick, John Macduff 51
Dickens, Charles 111
Distillers' Company 90
Dodwell, Henry 110
Domesday Survey 16,17, 18,49
Dundee Villa 62,*62*,69
Dunnett, coachman *43*
Dunstable Common 30,80
East and West Molesey
  UDC 61,62
East Molesey:
  acreage 9
  Building Society 31
  Common 80
  Cooperative Society 31
  Court 63,82,90
  Fire Brigade 4,70,71
  Local Board 61,62,67, 68,90,112

Lodge 88,89,92,*93*
  parish of 29,50
  Park 20,30,78,90
  police station 72
  Urban District Council .. 61
electric supply 30,66,67
Elm Lodge 91
Elmbridge:
  Borough 62,92
  Hundred 59
Ember:
  Court 81
  Mill 80,*84*
  River 13,30,*34*
Esher 14,20,24,29
  UDC 62
etymology *16*
Evans, Sarah 111
Faraday House Electrical College 92
Feltham, James 29
Field, Messrs J.C. & C. 82,*85*,91
fire brigade 4,30,68
  station 61,70,71
Fitzgilbert, Richard 17,18
flint arrowhead *12*,14
floods 14,30,31,32,33,43, 72,73,83,*107*
footbridge *75*
football 30,47
Foresters 31
Fox, Bishop 21,50
Frederick, Sir Thomas 110
Frederica, Princess *58*
Freeman, Ralph 18
Frithwald 15
gas supply 30,67
Goddard, John 109
Goodman, Alfred 90
Grange, The 91,*98*
gravel extraction 82
Graves, Mr (baker) 68
Griffen, J.J. & Sons 82
Grove, The 50,92,*101*,*102*
Guardians 60
gunpowder 81,89
Hale and Platts Charity *63*
Hall, Rev Alfred 51
  Samuel Carter 69
Hampton Court: 18,19,23, 24,29,80,81,89
  Bridge *3*,67,76,110
  Chase 18,19,23,24
  ferry 109
  Gas Company 67
  hare warren 23
  Palace 25,30,81,111
  Station 26,27,28, 42,43,76,80
handbill, 1858 .... *16*
  1821 .... *22*
Hansler, George Langley .. 29
Harper, Rev George 52
Hawkins, Thomas 81
Heirsey, William 112
Henneage, Sir Thomas . 19,89
Hersham 14
Higgins, D. 71
High House *104*
highwaymen 110
highways .... 60 et seq
hockey 30
Hodge, Lt F. 70
Hollis, William 109

Holly Lodge *93*
Horticultural Society 31
hospitals 31,60,69,72
Hotham, Beaumont Lord . 18 19,92,113
  Colonel 92
Howard, Donald Gordon .. 30
  Houses 30,*37*
hundreds 59
Hurst, The 30
  House 20,90,*93*
  Park Racing Club 90
Hurstside 91
inclosure 79,80
Iron Age *12*,14
Island Barn 30,*40*,*41*
  Farm 30,*40*
Ivy Cottage 91
  Lodge 92,*102*
Jesse, Edward 27,*100*
  John Henneage 27
John 18
Jones, Jenkin 92
Jubilee Fountain *73*
Jury, Messrs A. & F. 91
Kent, Francis Jackson .. 27, 28,50,67
  Estate catalogue *123*
  Mr (chemist) 68
  Town 27,67
King, Thomas 81
Kings: Athelstan 15
  Charles I 18
  Edgar 15
  Edward the Confessor .. 15
  Edward VI 24
  Edwy 15
  George IV 19
  Henry VIII 18,19,23
  John 80
  William the Conqueror .. 17
Kingston Rural Sanitary Authority 61
Knapp, Drewitt & Sons ... 126
Knox, Dr *43*,63
Lambeth Water Company 67,112
Launder, Alexander 51
Lawrence, John 113
Le Fullack 79
library 69
Limes, The 91,*99*
Lincoln, Alfred 71
Littlehales, Baker John 19
local government .... 59 et seq
Lodge, The, East Molesey . 29
  West Molesey .. 91,*103*,*104*
log canoes *12*,14
Long Ditton 68
Lorne Cottage *104*
Lot Mead 80
Lovibond, Edward 110
Lyceum Hall 66
Lydmore Shott 79
Lytcott, Sir John 18
Manor of Molesey
  Matham ..... 18 et seq,*20*,80
  of Molesey Prior . 19 et seq, 21,80
  Court 20,91
  Book *20*
  courts 59
  Farm, East Molesey 19, 21,*26*,28

124

West Molesey 30,*41*
House, Matham 20,28
  Prior 19,*21*,29
  West Molesey 20,*91*
Marryatt, Capt 92
Matham, John de 18
Merton Priory 19,80
Metropolitan Police 68,*72*
Mills:
  East Molesey 26
  Ember 80,*84*
  Lower, or Sterte *42,78*,
                             80,81,*83*
  Upper *78*,80,81
Mole Abbey (Mole Cottage,
  Mole Lodge *95,96,97*
  Abbey Cottage 91,*97*
  Bridge 74
  River 13,14,27,30,*42*,
       44,59,79,80,82,89,90,110
Molesey:
  acreage 9
  Boat Club 30
  Cottage Hospital 72
  Football Club 91
  Hurst Golf Club 30
  Isabella de 18
  Labour Party 52
  Liberal Party 28,61
  Mechanics Band 45
  name, derivation of 16
  Sampson de 18,80
  Souvenir *126*
  UDC 67
  Youth Club *107*
Monk's Pool 92
Moss Hall 51
Motcombe *31*
Moulsey Villa 92
Mul 15
Nielson, Christian 81
  Playing Field 80
Nitingale, Parnell 109
Norman, James 81,110
Oatlands 23
Oddfellows 31
Old Manor House,
  East Molesey 20,82,*84*
  West Molesey 20,*22*,
                              99,*100*
Olde Home *114*
omnibus 111
Paddock, The 113
Paine, Thomas 90
Palmer, family 90,92
  Joseph (Budworth) ... 90,91
parish officers .... 60 et seq
Pelloe, Rev Ebenezer *53*
Payne, E. *87*
Pemberton, William 28
Pitcher, Philip 68
police box *66*
Polfurlong 79
poor law 60
Post Offices:
  East Molesey 68,111
  West Molesey 68,111
Potterton and Gould 82
Powell, Anthony 109
Poyntz, Miss (Lady Clinton) 30
Priory, The 82,*85*,91,110
Public houses:
  Albion 68,111,*115*
  Bell ... 60,61,68,69,109,110
  Bridge Coffee House . 110,
                           111,*114*

Cannon 112,*119*
Carnarvon Castle 111,
              112,113,*118*,*119*
Castle 3,26,60,*108*,109,
        110,111,*113,114,118*
Europa 28,30,112,*116*
Ferryboat Inn 110,113,
                         118,119
King's Arms 60,110,111
Lord Hotham 113
New Inn 26,112,*115*
Paddock 113
Poyntz Arms 30,67,112,
                             113,*116*
Prince of Wales .. 3,111,*115*
Railway Hotel 111
Royal Oak 60,68,109,
                       111,112,*120*
Streets of London 113
Surveyor 113,*121*
Swan 60,109
Thames Hotel 112,113,
                            117,118
Traveller's Friend 112
Village Arms 113
White Hart 109,112
Quillets Royal 109
Radnor House *94*
railway 50,111
Ray's Charity *64*
Regatta 30
reservoirs 67
  Bessborough 92
  Island Barn 30,*40*,66
Reynolds, John 23
  William 23
Roads, etc:
  Anne Way 82
  Arnison Road *54,75*,90
  Avern Road 30,82
  Balmoral Crescent *37*
  Beauchamp Road 91
  Bell Road 20,29,30,51,
                        60,82,89,*105*
  Brende Gardens 91,*98*
  Bridge Road 19,27,29,
      38,51,52,54,68,*73,86*,
      87,90,*104*,110,111,112,
                     118,119,126
  Bridge Row 111
  Cannon Way 30,*41*
  Cedar Road 19,89
  Central Avenue 82
  Central Parade 68
  Creek Road *43*
  Dene, The 92,*103*
  Dennis (Dennes) Road ... 28
  Down Street 30
  Eastcote Ave 51
  Esher Road 29,*34,35,36*,
                             74,110
  Feltham Avenue 66,112
  Grange Road 30,*33*,91
  Green Lane 84
  Grove Road 75
  Hampton Court Ave ... *36*
  Helen Close 82
  High Street 20,30,*42*,68,
               69,79,80,91,*104*,112
  Hurst Lane 27,28
  Hurst Road 23,30,*32*,79,
                          80,90,91,*107*
  Island Farm Road 82
  Keen's Alley 27
  Kent Road 28,*32*
  Langton Road 30,*34*

Manor Road 28,29,51,
                             67,69
Matham Road 20,28,61,
                             67,68
Mole Abbey Gardens *95*
Molesey Park Road 90
Molesey Road 92
New Road 68,*74*,90,*95*,107
Palace Road 28,*31*
Park Road 28,29,52,68
Pemberton Road 28,*35*,
                             69,*72*
Portsmouth Road 110
Priory Lane 30
River Bank *105*,112
St Mary's Road 62,69
School Road 19,29
Seymour Road 68,89
Spencer Road 68
Spreighton (Spreyton)
  Road 30,*38*
Spring Gardens 82
Summer Road *43*,75
Tonbridge Road *39*,92,
                             102
Vine Road 28,52,61
Walton Road 19,*26*,27,
       29,*30*,31,*32*,52,61,62,
       67,68,*74*,79,87,89,91,
           92,*94*,110,*106*,112
Wilton Gardens 91
Windsor Avenue *37*
Wolsey Road 28,*106*
Robert Vince Advertising 81
Rose Cottages 92
Rowe and Stevens (drapers) 68
Rowlls, Mr 110
Sadler, James 91
Salter, Edward 90
  Stephen 50
  Talford 90
St Andrew's Hall *76*
  Eloy's Farm 109
  George's Bridge *41*
  John Ambulance
    Brigade 68
  Mary's Junior Cricket
    Club *48*
  Paul's Football Club *47*
Samine, John 81
Sausmarez, Capt Lionel
  de, R.N. *93*
Sawbridgeworth, Herts 18
Schools:
  Bishop Fox 30
  East Molesey Boys' *97*
  Girl's 69,*75*
  John Nightingale 30
  St Mary's 29
  St Paul's 29
  West Molesey *45,47*,77
scouts *46*
sewerage 30
Seymour, Sir Horace
  Beauchamp 30
Shairp, Sir Stephen 92
Shaw, Willam 111
Smyth, family 18,90
  Sir Robert 18,*21*,90
Spencer, Countess 30
Spinks, Frederick Lowton . 89
Standard Chartered
  Bank 80,90,*94*
Stanfurlong 79
Stoke d'Abernon 18,62
Stone Age 14

Stonyhurst 52
Strawberry Villa 90
Summers, The 30
  Farm 30
Sumner, J.W. 61
Surrey County Council ... 61
Sutton Lodge (Villa) 92
  Sir Richard 91
  Thomas 18,19
Sydenham, Rev E.A. 51
Tagg, Harry 52,112
Tagg's Island 13,67
Tanner's Bridge 11,*78*,82,
                             109
tannery 82,*84*
Taylor, John 68,109
  Mrs 68
telephone 30,67,68
Thames
  River 13,14,15,27,82,
                       89,91,110
  Ditton 24,29,59,80
Thomas, Thomas 51
Thompson, Sir Henry .. 91,*96*
Thorowgood, Frances 51
tithes 80
Toco 15
Todd, Joseph 89
Tonbridge, Richard de 17
Tor House 51
Tovi 15
Trafalgar House Group ... 80
Trollop and Colls 90
Ullward 15
Upper Farm 30
Usher, Thomas
  (ironmonger) 68,*87*
Vicarage, East Molesey *54*
  West Molesey *56,100*
Vine, Henry 28
Wales, Princess of 30
Wallace, Mr (draper) 68
Walnut Tree House *88*,89
Walpole, Horace 89
  Lt Gen Sir Robert *102*
Walton-on-Thames 14,
                                24,62
water splash *43*
  supply 30
Watford, Herts 82
Waverley Cottage 69
Weasen, Francis 81
Wells, Edmund Lionel 91
West Molesey:
  acreage 9
  Church-Warden's
    Accounts Book *64*
  Parish Council 60
  Parish pump 25
  views of *33*,*105*,*126*
  War memorial 74
Westminster Freehold
  Land Society 28
Weybridge 24,62,81,111
Whiteside, H.S. & Co. 82
Wilderness, The 90,*94*
Wimbledon Common 14
Wood, Mr Harry *116*
Woodbine Cottage 35
Wolsey, Cardinal 19,23,*25*,89
workhouse 60
Working Men's Club 31
Wulfhere 15
Wyndham, William 91

Zenith Motor Company 81

125

Tailpiece: Knapp, Drewitt and Sons Ltd of East Molesey produced this 1930s postcard, showing Bridge Road and West Molesey, topping and tailing the coat of arms — a Souvenir of Molesey.

ENDPAPERS: Detail from Rocque's Map of Surrey, c1768.

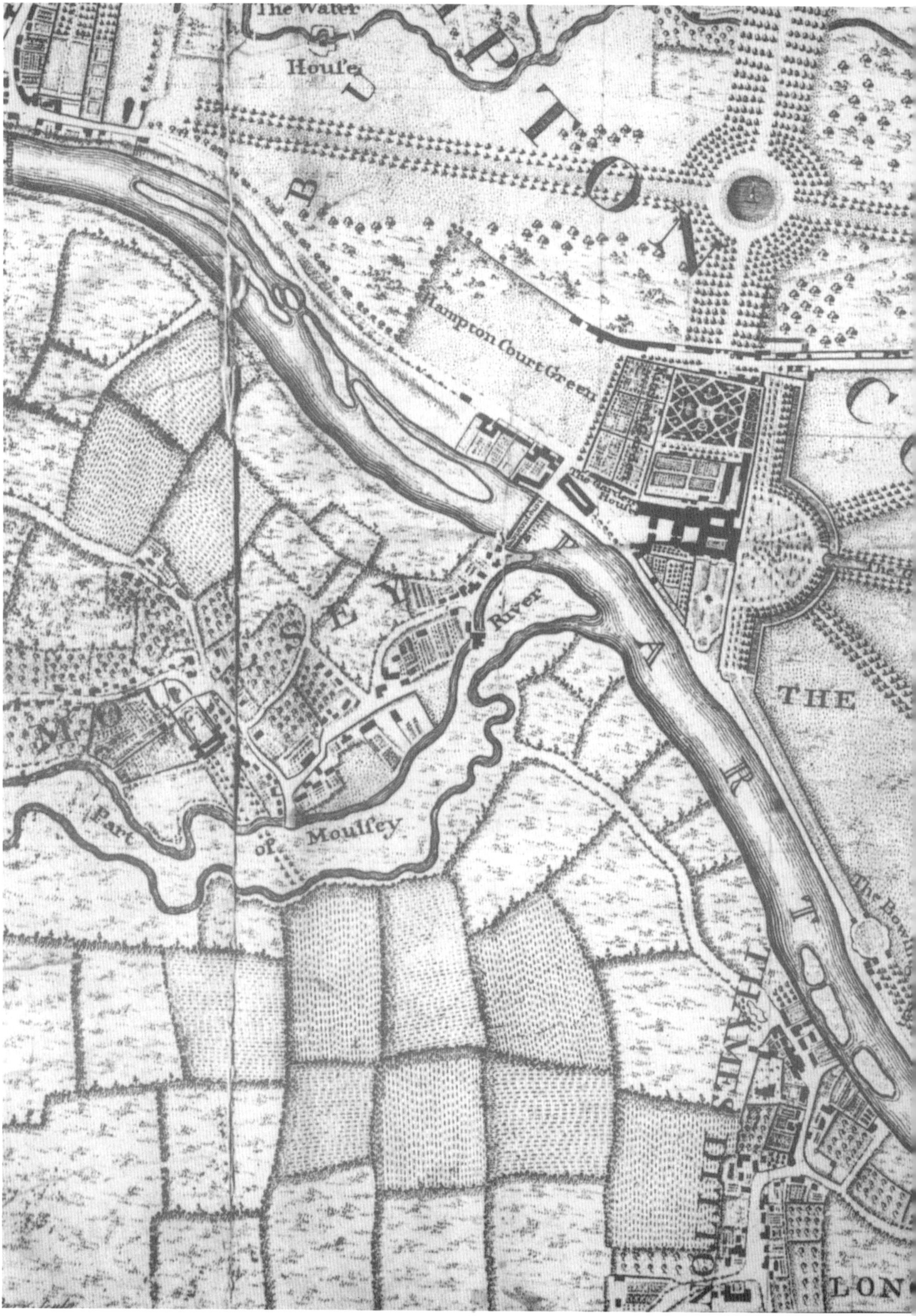
The Water
House
Hampton Court Green
River
Part
of Moulsey
THE